FOUR SEASONS
IN PLASTIC CANVAS

Dazzling winter snowflakes ... cheery spring flowers ... warm summer accents ... rich autumn color. That's what this exciting collection of plastic canvas projects is all about — helping you celebrate all that life has to offer by filling your home with the beauty of the seasons. Inside this handy keepsake book, you'll find more than 80 projects to mark the year's changes and decorate for the holidays. The pretty wall hangings that introduce each section can be displayed individually in a favorite spot and interchanged as each season arrives — or you can hang them all together the whole year-round. Creating an inviting atmosphere for your home has never been easier!

LEISURE ARTS, INC.
Little Rock, Arkansas

FOUR SEASONS IN PLASTIC CANVAS
BOOK SIX

EDITORIAL STAFF

Vice President and Editor-in-Chief:
Anne Van Wagner Childs
Executive Director: Sandra Graham Case
Executive Editor: Susan Frantz Wiles
Publications Director: Carla Bentley
Creative Art Director: Gloria Bearden
Production Art Director: Melinda Stout

PRODUCTION
Managing Editor: Lisa Truxton Curton
Senior Editor: Donna Brown Hill
Project Coordinators: Phyllis Miller Boorsma,
Michelle Sass Goodrich, Becky Guthrie, Catherine
Hubmann, Susan McManus Johnson, and Rhonda
Goerke Lombardo
Project Assistant: Kandi Brock Ashford

DESIGN
Design Director: Patricia Wallenfang Sowers

EDITORIAL
Associate Editor: Linda L. Trimble
Senior Editorial Writer: Darla Burdette Kelsay
Editorial Associates: Tammi Williamson Bradley,
Terri Leming Davidson, and Robyn Sheffield-Edwards
Copy Editor: Laura Lee Weland

ART
Crafts Art Director: Rhonda Hodge Shelby
Senior Production Artist: Jonathan M. Flaxman
Production Artists: Roberta Aulwes, Mary Ellen
Wilhelm, Katie Murphy, Dana Vaughn, Michael A.
Spigner, Hubrith E. Esters, Karen L. Wilson, and
Gregory A. Needels
Photography Stylists: Emily Minnick, Christina Tiano
Myers, Sondra Daniel, Aurora Huston, and
Laura Bushmiaer

BUSINESS STAFF

Publisher: Bruce Akin
Vice President, Finance: Tom Siebenmorgen
Vice President, Retail Sales: Thomas L. Carlisle
Retail Sales Director: Richard Tignor
Vice President, Retail Marketing: Pam Stebbins
Retail Customer Services Director: Margaret Sweetin

Marketing Manager: Russ Barnett
Executive Director of Marketing and Circulation:
Guy A. Crossley
Circulation Manager: Byron L. Taylor
Print Production Manager: Laura Lockhart
Print Production Coordinator: Nancy Reddick Lister

Library of Congress Catalog Number 95-78898
Hardcover ISBN 0-942237-87-0
Softcover ISBN 0-942237-88-9

TABLE OF CONTENTS

WINTER

One of the most widely recognized symbols of the season, the evergreen stands triumphant over the cold, dark days of winter. The majestic trees slumber under a starry sky on our enchanting wall hanging and tissue box cover. Taken from the quilt-block border, the coordinating magnet carries out the tranquil colors. This wintry set, along with the other projects in this collection featuring redbirds, sleigh ride scenes, and more, will help you celebrate the beauty of winter and the joys of Christmas.

With their bright plumage, cardinals have long been harbingers of the holiday season. Our redbird magnets (right) will add a festive note to your message center. Fashioned to resemble a bird feeder, our tissue box cover (opposite) captures the cheery birds enjoying a leisurely winter snack. The coordinating picture frame (below) is perfect for displaying a favorite Christmas photograph.

Cap off a cold winter's evening with a steaming cup of cocoa served in our bargello mug. The pretty zigzag pattern gets its festive flair from rich shades of red and green contrasted with ecru. Depicting a charming sleigh ride scene, the picturesque throw rug is worked with fabric strips on 5 mesh plastic canvas.

Our handy fireplace match holder, created using traditional bargello needlepoint, is designed to hang on the wall. Topped with a sleigh motif that coordinates with the rug, the playing card box holds two decks of poker-size cards.

Our shimmering tree ornament (right) personifies the beauty of a single snowflake. The ornament works up quickly on white 7 mesh plastic canvas, so why not stitch up a flurry of them! A photo album (below) dressed in our four seasons cover makes a thoughtful Christmas gift that will be enjoyed all year-round. It's a wonderful place to store family photographs and other treasured mementos. Perfect for greeting your holiday guests, our Santa door decoration (opposite) portrays the jolly old gentleman heralding the season with a golden horn.

NL COLOR

☒ 14 brown - 12 yds

☑ 17 gold - 11 yds

NL COLOR

☑ 24 lt green - 11 yds

☒ 29 green - 23 yds

NL COLOR

☒ 30 olive green - 16 yds

☑ 39 ecru - 100 yds

NL COLOR

☒ 42 burgundy - 18 yds

INSTRUCTIONS ARE ON PAGE 14.

Top Section

Wall Hanging (81 x 121 threads)

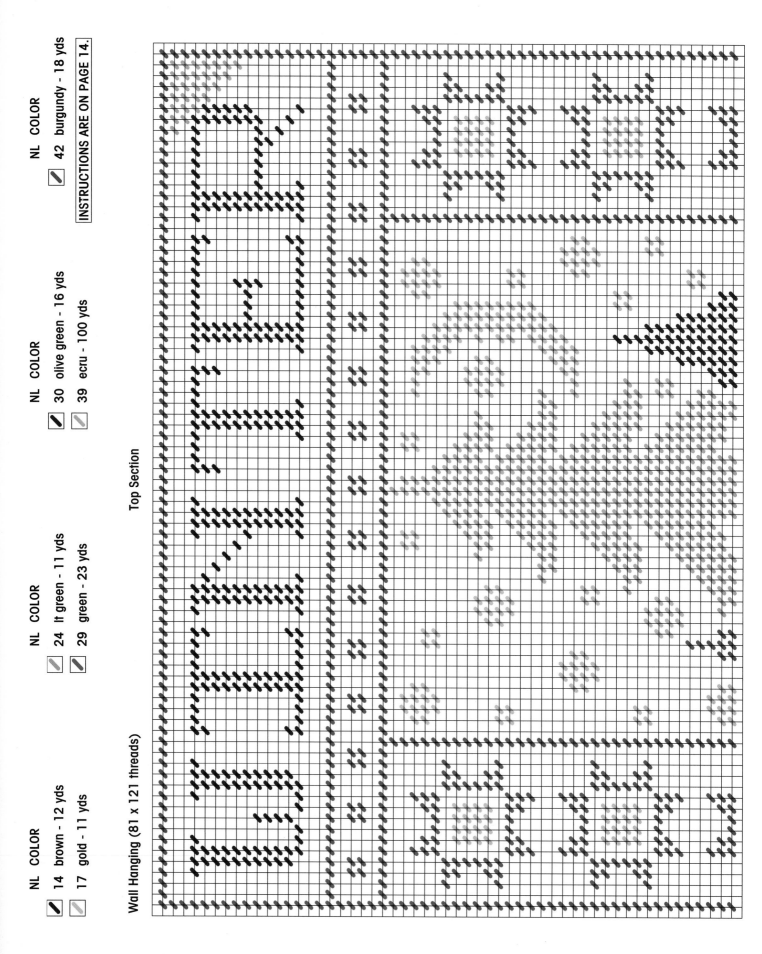

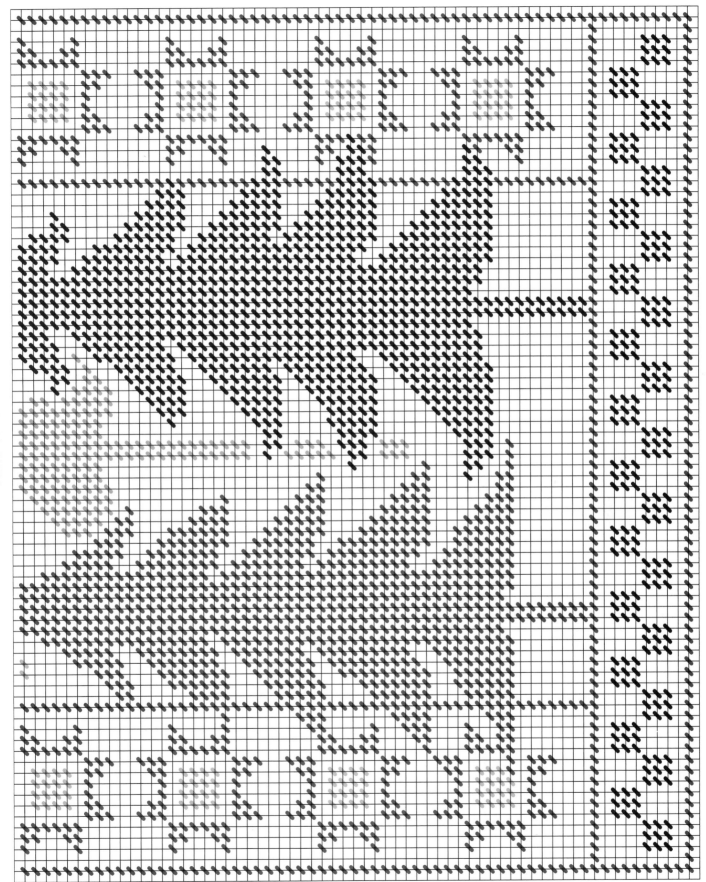

WINTER WALL HANGING
Skill Level: Intermediate
Size: 12"w x 18"h
Supplies: Needloft® Plastic Canvas Yarn or worsted weight yarn (refer to color key), one 12" x 18" sheet of 7 mesh plastic canvas, #16 tapestry needle, sewing needle and thread, and sawtooth hanger
Stitches Used: Overcast Stitch and Tent Stitch
Instructions: Photo model was stitched using Needloft® Plastic Canvas Yarn. (**Note:** Design fits a 12" x 18" sheet of canvas.) Follow chart and use required stitches to work Top Section. Follow chart and use required stitches to work Bottom Section below Top Section. Complete background with ecru Tent Stitches as indicated on chart. Use ecru Overcast Stitches to cover unworked edges. Use sewing needle and thread to attach sawtooth hanger to wrong side of stitched piece.

WINTER TISSUE BOX COVER
Skill Level: Beginner
Size: 4½"w x 5¾"h x 4½"d
(**Note:** Fits a 4¼"w x 5¼"h x 4¼"d boutique tissue box.)
Supplies: Needloft® Plastic Canvas Yarn or worsted weight yarn (refer to color key), one 10½" x 13½" sheet of 7 mesh plastic canvas, and #16 tapestry needle
Stitches Used: Overcast Stitch and Tent Stitch
Instructions: Photo model was stitched using Needloft® Plastic Canvas Yarn. Follow charts and use required stitches to work Tissue Box Cover pieces. Complete backgrounds with ecru Tent Stitches as indicated on charts. Use green for all joining. Join Sides along long edges. Join Top to Sides.

WINTER MAGNET
Skill Level: Beginner
Size: 2⅜"w x 2⅜"h
Supplies: Needloft® Plastic Canvas Yarn or worsted weight yarn (refer to color key), one 10½" x 13½" sheet of 7 mesh plastic canvas, #16 tapestry needle, magnetic strip, and clear-drying craft glue
Stitches Used: Overcast Stitch and Tent Stitch
Instructions: Photo model was stitched using Needloft® Plastic Canvas Yarn. Follow chart and use required stitches to work Magnet. Glue magnetic strip to wrong side of stitched piece.

Winter Set designs by Polly Carbonari.

NL	COLOR	
	17	gold - 12 yds
	24	lt green - 13 yds
	29	green - 20 yds
	39	ecru - 55 yds

Magnet (16 x 16 threads)

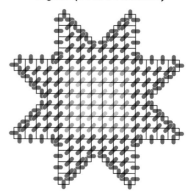

Tissue Box Cover Side (30 x 38 threads) (Work 4)

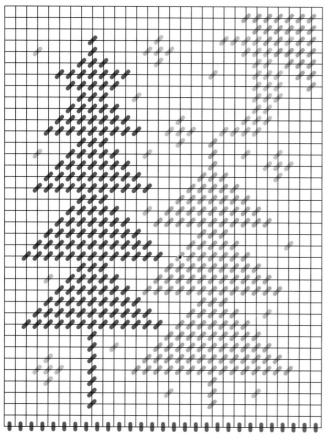

Tissue Box Cover Top (30 x 30 threads)

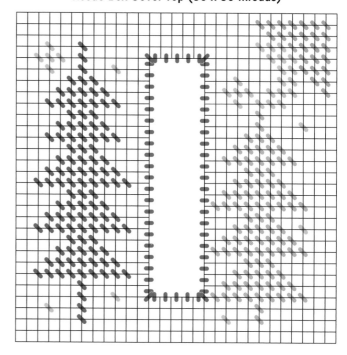

PICTURE FRAME

Skill Level: Intermediate

Size: 6⅜"w x 10"h

(**Note:** Photo opening is 4¾"w x 6¾"h.)

Supplies: Worsted weight yarn or Needloft® Plastic Canvas Yarn (refer to color key), two 10½" x 13½" sheets of 7 mesh white plastic canvas, #16 tapestry needle, and sewing needle and thread

Stitches Used: French Knot, Gobelin Stitch, Overcast Stitch, Scotch Stitch, and Tent Stitch

Instructions: Photo model was stitched using worsted weight yarn. Follow charts and use required stitches to work Picture Frame pieces. For Back, cut a piece of plastic canvas 38 x 54 threads. For Stand Top, cut a piece of plastic canvas 14 x 52 threads. For Stand Bottom, cut a piece of plastic canvas 14 x 20 threads. (**Note:** Back, Stand Top, and Stand Bottom are not worked.) Refer to photo for placement and use red to tack Holly to Front. Refer to Diagram and use white for remainder of joining. Join Stand Top to Stand Bottom along one short edge. Center and join short unworked edge of Stand Top to one short edge of Back. Center and join short unworked edge of Stand Bottom to remaining short edge of Back. Center Back over photo opening on wrong side of Front. Use sewing needle and thread to tack Back to Front along sides and bottom of Back.

Picture Frame design by Dick Martin.

NL	COLOR	
▨	02	red - 1 yd
▨	41	white - 15 yds
▨	53	green - 10 yds
●	41	white Fr. Knot

Front (71 x 71 threads)

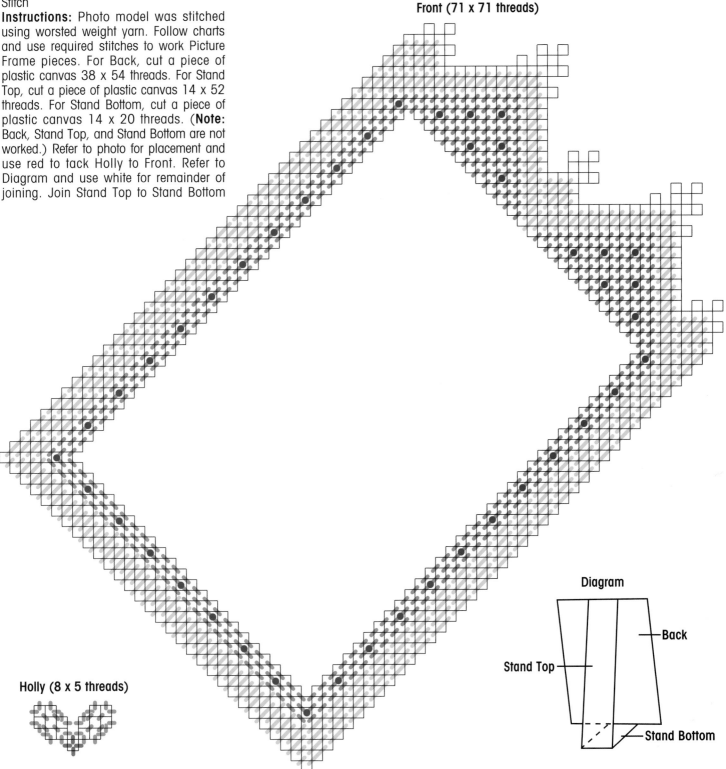

Diagram

Back

Stand Top

Stand Bottom

Holly (8 x 5 threads)

BIRD FEEDER TISSUE BOX COVER

Skill Level: Intermediate
Size: 4⅞"w x 6⅞"h x 4⅞"d
(**Note:** Fits a 4¼"w x 4¾"h x 4¼"d boutique tissue box.)
Supplies: Worsted weight yarn or Needloft® Plastic Canvas Yarn (refer to color key), one 10½" x 13½" sheet of clear 7 mesh plastic canvas, three 10½" x 13½" sheets of white 7 mesh plastic canvas, and #16 tapestry needle
Stitches Used: Backstitch, French Knot, Gobelin Stitch, Overcast Stitch, and Tent Stitch
Instructions: Photo model was stitched using worsted weight yarn. Cut Sides and Top from white plastic canvas. Cut remaining pieces from clear plastic canvas. Follow charts and use required stitches to work Tissue Box Cover pieces, leaving stitches in shaded areas unworked. Use white to join Sides along long edges. Work stitches in shaded areas to join Top to Sides. Refer to photo for placement to assemble pieces. Use green to tack two Holly pieces to each Garland. Use green to tack Garland pieces to Top. Use red to tack remaining Holly pieces to Sides. Use yarn color to match stitching area to tack Cardinals to Sides.

Bird Feeder Tissue Box Cover design by Dick Martin.

CARDINAL MAGNETS

Skill Level: Beginner
Approx Size: 2¼"w x 2"h each
Supplies: Worsted weight yarn or Needloft® Plastic Canvas Yarn (refer to color key), one 10½" x 13½" sheet of clear 7 mesh plastic canvas, #16 tapestry needle, magnetic strip, and clear-drying craft glue
Stitches Used: Backstitch, French Knot, Gobelin Stitch, Overcast Stitch, and Tent Stitch
Instructions: Photo models were stitched using worsted weight yarn. Follow chart and use required stitches to work desired Cardinal. Glue magnetic strip to wrong side of stitched piece.

Cardinal Magnet designs by Dick Martin.

NL COLOR

	NL	COLOR
✎	00	black - 2 yds
✎	02	red - 5 yds
✎	09	dk gold - 4 yds
✎	12	gold - 4 yds
✎	41	white - 35 yds
✎	53	green - 40 yds
✎	58	orange - 1 yd
●		white Fr. Knot*
●		ecru Fr. Knot* - 2 yds

*Use 2-ply yarn.

Cardinal #1 (15 x 13 threads) (Work 2)

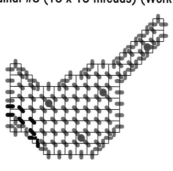

Cardinal #2 (15 x 13 threads) (Work 2)

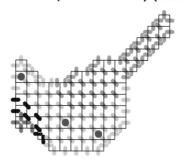

Garland (16 x 16 threads) (Work 2)

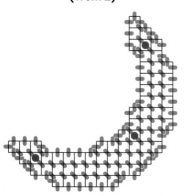

Cardinal #3 (15 x 13 threads) (Work 2)

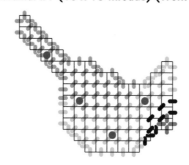

Cardinal #4 (15 x 19 threads) (Work 2)

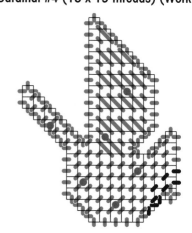

Top (44 x 44 threads)

Holly (8 x 7 threads)
(Work 8)

Side (50 x 50 threads) (Work 4)

17

BARGELLO FIREPLACE MATCH HOLDER

Skill Level: Beginner
Size: 3"w x 13⅜"h x 1⅝"d
Stitches Used: Gobelin Stitch and Overcast Stitch
Supplies: Worsted weight yarn or Needloft® Plastic Canvas Yarn (refer to color key), one 10½" x 13½" sheet of 7 mesh plastic canvas, one 3" dia plastic canvas circle, and #16 tapestry needle

Instructions: Photo model was stitched using 2 strands of worsted weight yarn. Follow chart to cut Bottom from 3" dia plastic canvas circle. Follow charts and use required stitches to work Bargello Fireplace Match Holder pieces. Use a double thickness of canvas for Back. Use green for all joining. Match ★'s and ■'s to join Front to Back. Match ▲'s to join Bottom to Front and Back.

Bargello Fireplace Match Holder design by Teal Lee Elliott.

Bottom

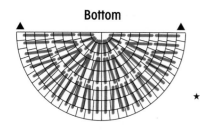

NL	COLOR
03	red - 25 yds
29	green - 40 yds
39	ecru - 27 yds

Front (32 x 70 threads)

Back (20 x 89 threads)

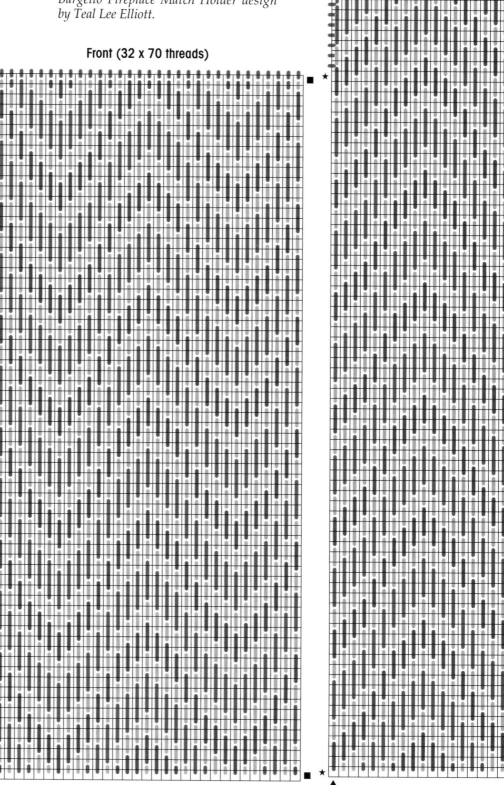

18

PLAYING CARD HOLDER

Skill Level: Beginner
Size: 6¾"w x 4½"h x 1¼"d
Stitches: Backstitch, Cross Stitch, Overcast Stitch, and Tent Stitch
Supplies: Worsted weight yarn or Needloft® Plastic Canvas Yarn (refer to color key), one 10½" x 13½" sheet of 7 mesh plastic canvas, and #16 tapestry needle
Instructions: Photo model was stitched using worsted weight yarn. Follow charts and use required stitches to work Playing Card Holder pieces. For Bottom, cut a piece of plastic canvas 42 x 28 threads. For Bottom Long Sides, cut two pieces of plastic canvas 42 x 7 threads each. For Bottom Short Sides, cut two pieces of plastic canvas 28 x 7 threads each. For Divider, cut a piece of plastic canvas 27 x 7 threads. Use ecru Tent Stitches to work Bottom, Bottom Long Sides, Bottom Short Sides, and Divider. Use ecru for all joining. Join Top Long Sides to Top Short Sides along short edges. Join Top to Top Sides. Join Bottom Long Sides to Bottom Short Sides along short edges. Join Bottom to Bottom Sides. Place Divider in center of Box Bottom. Use ecru to tack Divider to Bottom and Bottom Long Sides. Use ecru Overcast Stitches to cover unworked edges.

Playing Card Holder design by Polly Carbonari.

NL	COLOR	
	29	green - 35 yds
	39	ecru - 100 yds

Top Short Side
(30 x 7 threads)
(Work 2)

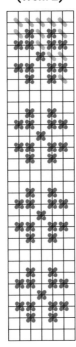

BARGELLO MUG INSERT

Skill Level: Beginner
Size: 3½"h x 3⅛" dia
Stitches Used: Gobelin Stitch and Overcast Stitch
Supplies: Worsted weight yarn (refer to color key), one 10½" x 13½" sheet of 10 mesh plastic canvas, green Crafter's Pride® Mugs Your Way™ mug, and #20 tapestry needle
Instructions: Photo model was stitched using worsted weight yarn. Follow chart and use required stitches to work Mug Insert, starting at left end of canvas. Refer to photo and repeat charted pattern until Mug Insert is completed. Use green to join Mug Insert along short edges, forming a cylinder. Place Mug Insert into Mugs Your Way™ mug, aligning joined edges with mug handle. Remove stitched piece before washing mug.

Bargello Mug Insert design by Teal Lee Elliott.

NL	COLOR	
	03	red - 6 yds
	29	green - 12 yds
	39	ecru - 10 yds

Top Long Side (44 x 7 threads) (Work 2)

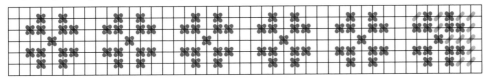

Top (44 x 30 threads)

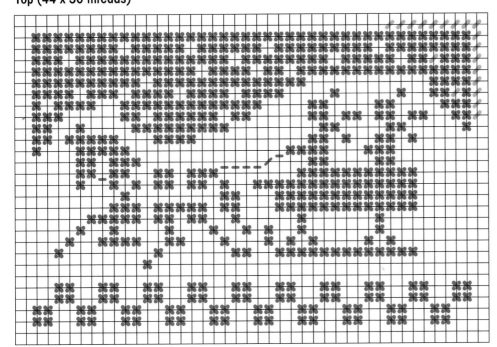

Mug Insert (95 x 36 threads)

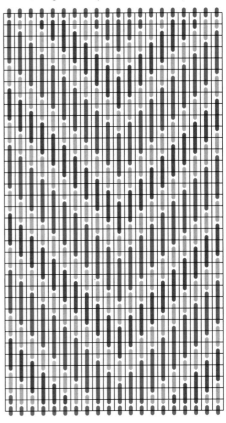

SLEIGH RIDE RUG

Skill Level: Intermediate

Size: 26"w x 16¾"h

Supplies: Two 13⅝" x 21⅝" sheets of 5 mesh plastic canvas, 44/45"w 100% cotton fabric (refer to photo and color key), #16 tapestry needle, non-skid rug backing (optional), and Scotchgard™ brand fabric protector (optional)

Stitches Used: Overcast Stitch and Tent Stitch

Instructions: Wash and press all fabrics. Cut off selvages. Tear fabric into ½"w x 44"l strips. Follow charts and use required stitches to work Rug pieces, leaving stitches in shaded areas unworked. Complete backgrounds with ecru Tent Stitches as indicated on charts. Match ▲'s and work stitches in shaded areas through two thicknesses to join Left Side to Right Side. Use green Overcast Stitches to cover

Left Side (67 x 84 threads)

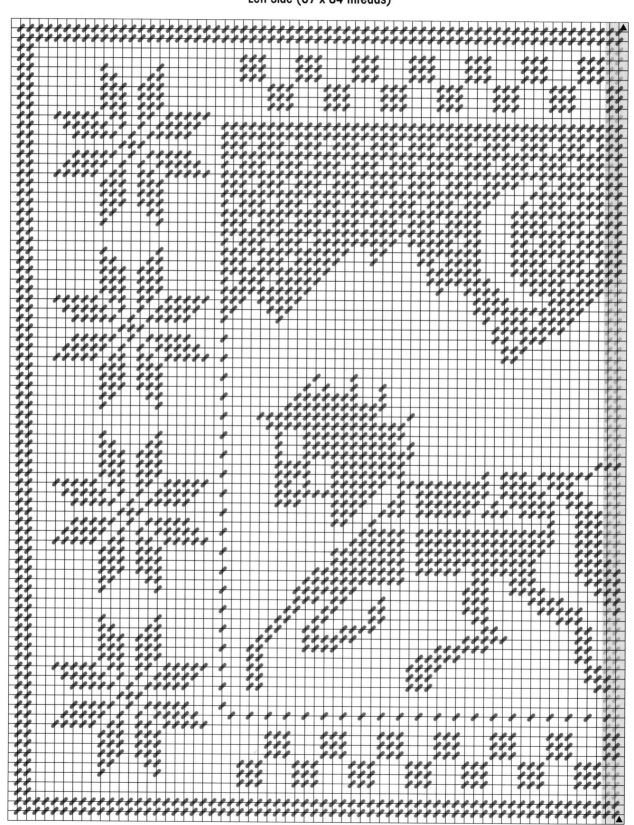

unworked edges. Follow manufacturer's instructions to apply Scotchgard™ brand fabric protector and non-skid backing to Rug.

Rug design by Polly Carbonari.

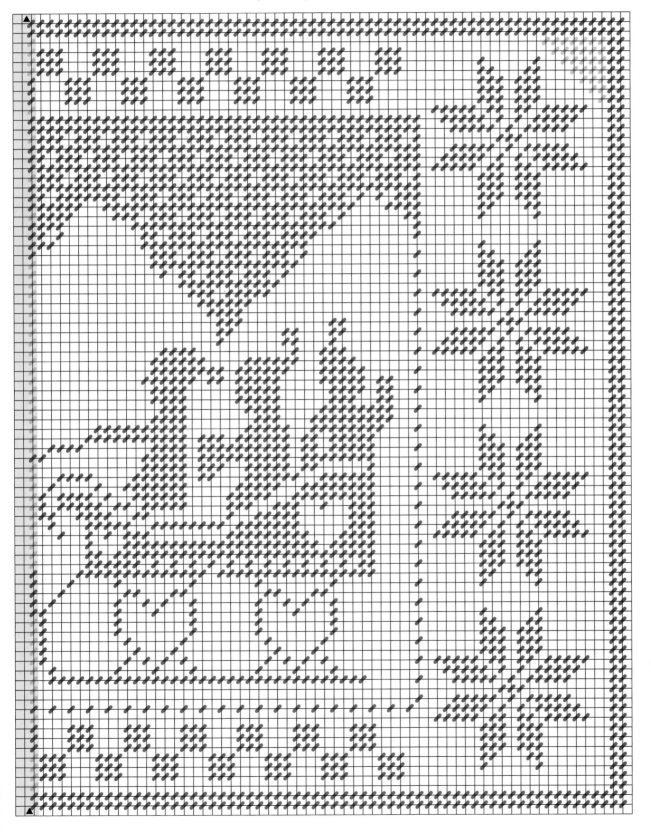

ecru - 2 yds

green - 1½ yds

Right Side (67 x 84 threads)

SNOWFLAKE ORNAMENT

Skill Level: Beginner
Size: 2⅞"w x 2⅞"h
Supplies: Worsted weight yarn or Needloft® Plastic Canvas Yarn (refer to color key), one 10½" x 13½" sheet of white 7 mesh plastic canvas, #16 tapestry needle, and nylon thread
Stitches Used: French Knot and Gobelin Stitch

Instructions: Photo model was stitched using worsted weight yarn. Follow chart and use required stitches to work Ornament. For hanger, thread 8" of nylon thread through stitched piece. Tie ends together in a knot 3" above Ornament.

Snowflake Ornament design by Dick Martin.

NL	COLOR	
▨	41	white - 4 yds
⊙	41	white Fr. Knot

Ornament (20 x 20 threads)

PHOTO ALBUM COVER

Skill Level: Intermediate
Size: 10¼"w x 12"h x 2⅝"d
(**Note:** Fits a 9¾"w x 11½"h photo album with 2" spine.)
Supplies: Worsted weight yarn or Needloft® Plastic Canvas Yarn (refer to color key), three 10½" x 13½" sheets of 7 mesh plastic canvas, #16 tapestry needle, and photo album
Stitches Used: Backstitch, French Knot, Gobelin Stitch, Mosaic Stitch, Overcast Stitch, and Tent Stitch

Instructions: Photo model was stitched using worsted weight yarn. Follow charts and use required stitches to work Photo Album Cover pieces. Work stitches indicated by double lines on chart by inserting needle in same holes twice for complete coverage. For Back, cut a piece of plastic canvas 68 x 80 threads. Use white Gobelin Stitches over three threads to work Back. Use white for all joining. With right sides facing up, join Front and Back to Spine along long edges. For Sleeves, cut two pieces of plastic canvas 15 x 80 threads each. Match corners of Sleeve to ▲'s on wrong side of Front to join Sleeve to Front. Repeat for Back and remaining Sleeve. Use white Overcast Stitches to cover unworked edges of Front, Back, and Spine.

Photo Album Cover design by Dick Martin.

NL	COLOR	
▨	00	black - 4 yds
▨		black*
▨	02	red - 25 yds
▨	11	gold - 1 yd
▨	21	yellow - 1 yd
▨	35	blue - 12 yds
▨	36	lt blue - 10 yds
▨	41	white - 85 yds
▨	48	dk blue - 7 yds
▨	53	green - 5 yds
⊙		white Fr. Knot*

*Use 2-ply yarn.

Spine (18 x 80 threads)

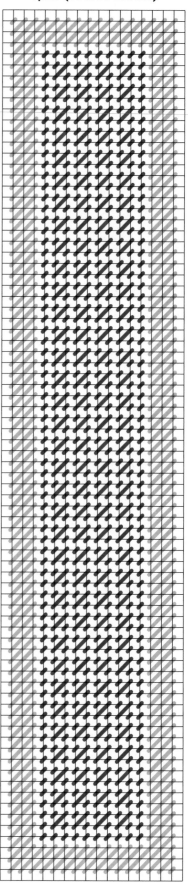

SANTA DOOR DECORATION

Skill Level: Beginner
Size: 13½"w x 28"h
Supplies: Worsted weight yarn or Needloft® Plastic Canvas Yarn (refer to color key), metallic gold cord (refer to color key), one 13⅝" x 22" sheet of clear 7 mesh plastic canvas, one 10½" x 13½" sheet of white 7 mesh plastic canvas, #16 tapestry needle, and nylon line

Stitches Used: Backstitch, Cross Stitch, French Knot, Gobelin Stitch, Mosaic Stitch, Overcast Stitch, Scotch Stitch, and Tent Stitch

Instructions: Photo model was stitched using worsted weight yarn. Cut Santa from 13⅝" x 22" sheet of plastic canvas. Cut Mustache, Holly, and Cardinals from clear plastic canvas. Cut Snowflakes from white plastic canvas. Follow charts and use required stitches to work Santa Door Decoration pieces. Refer to photo for placement and use red to tack one Cardinal to Santa. Use green to tack Holly to Santa. Match ▲'s and ✦'s and use white to tack Mustache to Santa. Use white to tack one Small Snowflake to Santa. Refer to Diagram and tie nylon line to pieces to assemble Santa Door Decoration.

Santa Door Decoration design by Dick Martin.

NL	COLOR
00	black - 1 yd
02	red - 25 yds
07	pink - 2 yds
27	green - 3 yds
41	white - 55 yds
48	blue - 23 yds
55	dk pink - 1 yd
56	flesh - 8 yds
58	orange - 1 yd
	metallic gold - 5 yds
41	white Fr. Knot

Small Snowflake (20 x 20 threads) (Work 4)

Holly (17 x 13 threads)

Large Snowflake (28 x 28 threads)

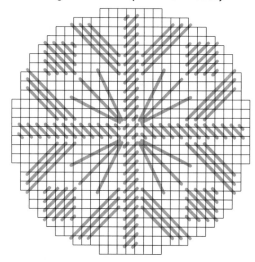

Cardinal (25 x 19 threads) (Work 2)

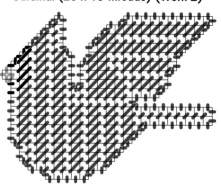

Mustache (25 x 17 threads)

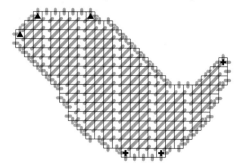

Diagram

- 1¾"
- ½"
- ½" — — ½"
- —3¼"

Santa (90 x 90 threads)

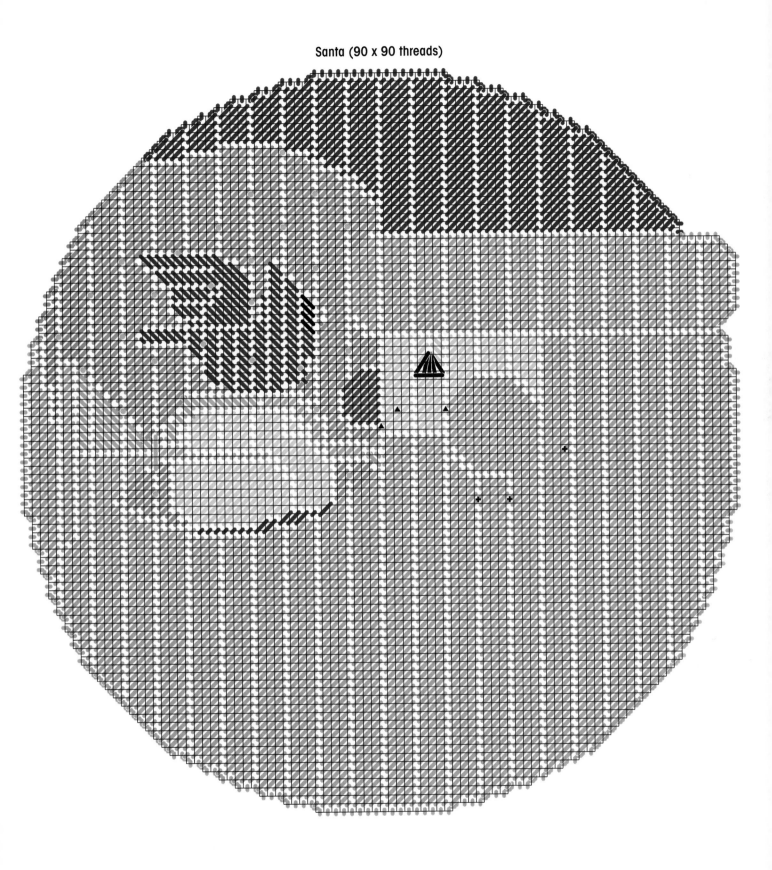

SPRING

Spring blooms anew each year, energizing our spirits with her gentle breezes and colorful blossoms. One of her best-loved flowers, the daffodil thrives forever on our pretty wall hanging and tissue box cover. The coordinating magnet from the quilt-block border continues the delightful look. The projects in this collection — from hummingbird magnets to a sweet little lamb basket — will fill you with the glory of spring and help you celebrate the promise of Easter.

A familiar sight in spring, the graceful hummingbird uses its long, slender bill to sip the nectar from deep-cupped flowers. We've captured their beauty on our bookend and coaster set (opposite). The matching magnets (left) *allow you to enjoy the red-throated birds on your message center. To complete the collection, a sweet sign* (below) *offers a charming blessing.*

Abloom with delicate color, this quaint country cottage (below) captures all the charm of spring. Dainty flowers and a white picket fence enhance the three-dimensional scene. Roses, created with dimensional rose stitches, lend a romantic air to our floral centerpiece holder (opposite). A border of six-trip herringbone stitches adds rich texture to the project.

This little lamb basket (right) *offers a sweet way to deliver happy Easter wishes. Filled with colorful jelly bean "eggs," our miniature Easter baskets* (below) *make precious party favors. Dressed in her Sunday best, our bunny door decoration* (opposite) *will greet your holiday guests with springtime charm.*

NL COLOR

☑ 11 orange - 10 yds
☑ 19 gold - 6 yds

NL COLOR

☑ 20 lt yellow - 3 yds
☑ 23 green - 9 yds

NL COLOR

☑ 25 lt green - 14 yds
☑ 35 blue - 15 yds

NL COLOR

☑ 39 ecru - 120 yds
☑ 53 aqua - 14 yds

NL COLOR

☑ 57 yellow - 9 yds

INSTRUCTIONS ARE ON PAGE 36.

Wall Hanging (81 x 121 threads)

Top Section

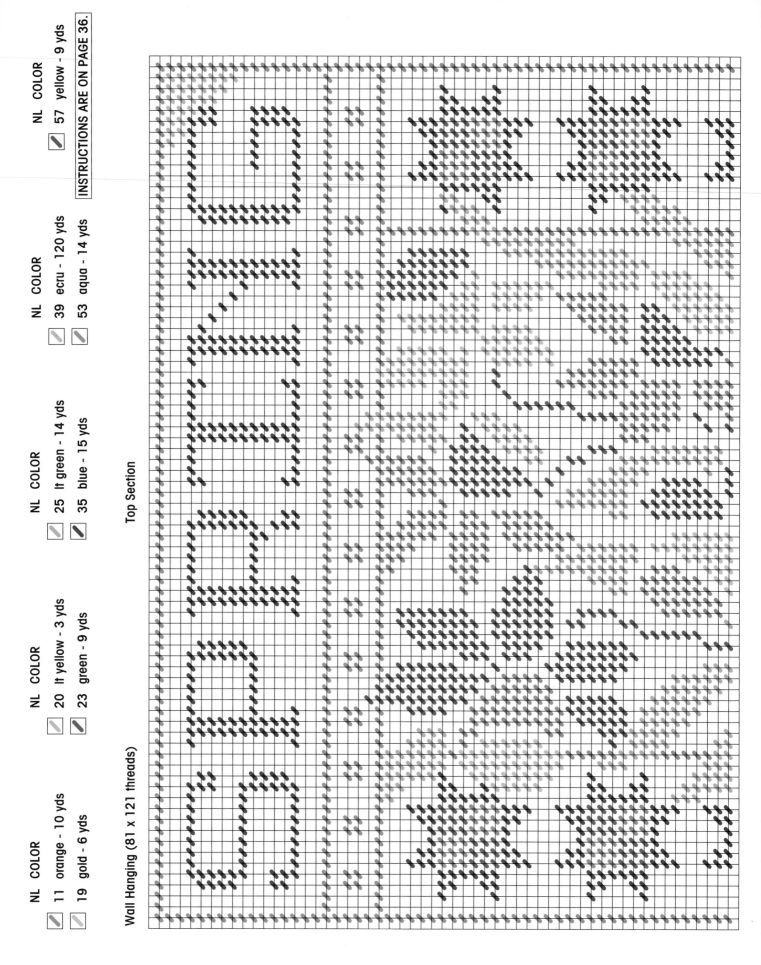

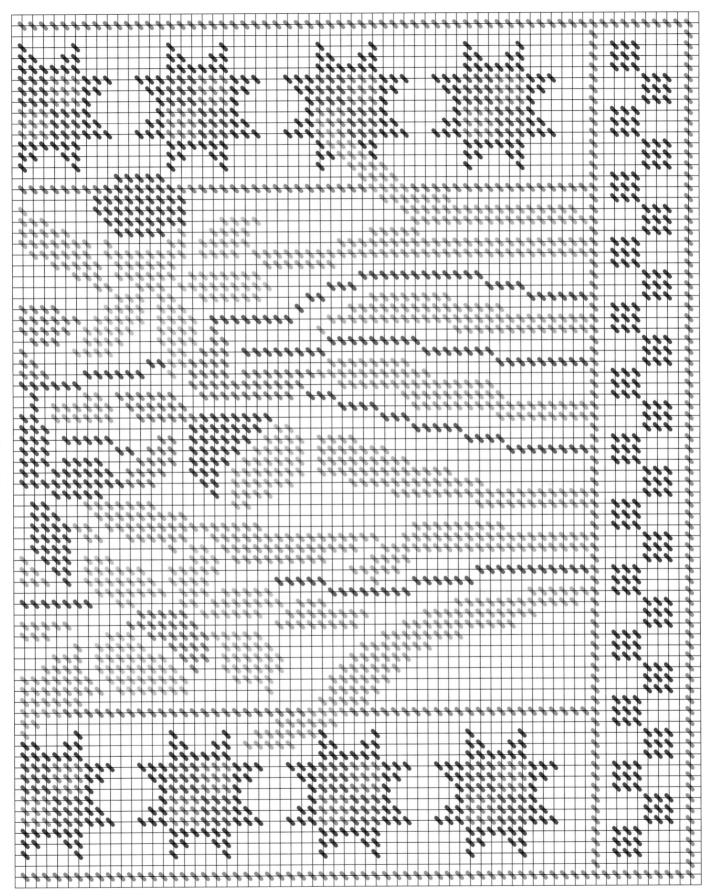

SPRING WALL HANGING

Skill Level: Intermediate
Size: 12"w x 18"h
Supplies: Needloft® Plastic Canvas Yarn or worsted weight yarn (refer to color key), one 12" x 18" sheet of 7 mesh plastic canvas, #16 tapestry needle, sewing needle and thread, and sawtooth hanger
Stitches Used: Overcast Stitch and Tent Stitch
Instructions: Photo model was stitched using Needloft® Plastic Canvas Yarn. (**Note:** Design fits a 12" x 18" sheet of canvas.) Follow chart and use required stitches to work Top Section. Follow chart and use required stitches to work Bottom Section below Top Section. Complete background with ecru Tent Stitches as indicated on chart. Use ecru Overcast Stitches to cover unworked edges. Use sewing needle and thread to attach sawtooth hanger to wrong side of stitched piece.

SPRING TISSUE BOX COVER

Skill Level: Beginner
Size: 4½"w x 5¾"h x 4½"d
(**Note:** Fits a 4¼"w x 5¼"h x 4¼"d boutique tissue box.)
Supplies: Needloft® Plastic Canvas Yarn or worsted weight yarn (refer to color key), one 10½" x 13½" sheet of 7 mesh plastic canvas, and #16 tapestry needle
Stitches Used: Overcast Stitch and Tent Stitch
Instructions: Photo model was stitched using Needloft® Plastic Canvas Yarn. Follow charts and use required stitches to work Tissue Box Cover pieces. Complete backgrounds with ecru Tent Stitches as indicated on charts. Use blue for all joining. Join Sides along long edges. Join Top to Sides.

SPRING MAGNET

Skill Level: Beginner
Size: 2"w x 2"h
Supplies: Needloft® Plastic Canvas Yarn or worsted weight yarn (refer to color key), one 10½" x 13½" sheet of 7 mesh plastic canvas, #16 tapestry needle, magnetic strip, and clear-drying craft glue
Stitches Used: Overcast Stitch and Tent Stitch
Instructions: Photo model was stitched using Needloft® Plastic Canvas Yarn. Follow chart and use required stitches to work Magnet. Glue magnetic strip to wrong side of stitched piece.

Spring Set designs by Polly Carbonari.

NL	COLOR		NL	COLOR
11	orange - 10 yds		25	lt green - 15 yds
19	gold - 6 yds		35	blue - 8 yds
20	lt yellow - 9 yds		39	ecru - 43 yds
23	green - 10 yds		57	yellow - 8 yds

Magnet (14 x 14 threads)

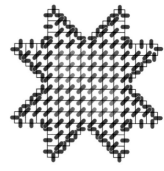

Tissue Box Cover Side (30 x 38 threads) (Work 4)

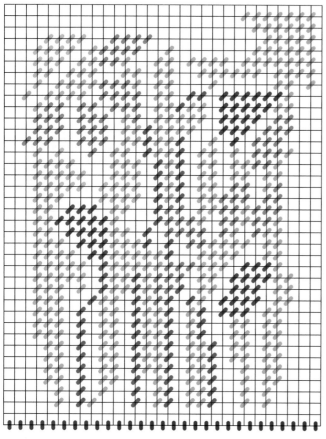

Tissue Box Cover Top (30 x 30 threads)

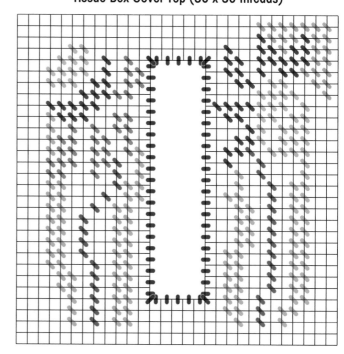

HUMMINGBIRD SET & "GOD BLESS OUR NEST" SIGN

(Note: Photo models were stitched using worsted weight yarn.)
Skill Level: Intermediate
Supplies for Entire Set: Worsted weight yarn or Needloft® Plastic Canvas Yarn (refer to color keys), six 10½" x 13½" sheets of 7 mesh plastic canvas, #16 tapestry needle, one brick, plastic wrap, cork or felt, magnetic strip, sewing needle and thread, sawtooth hanger, and clear-drying craft glue
Stitches Used: Alternating Mosaic Stitch, Backstitch, Cross Stitch, Gobelin Stitch, Overcast Stitch, Scotch Stitch, Smyrna Cross Stitch, and Tent Stitch

HUMMINGBIRD COASTER SET

Coaster Size: 4½"w x 4½"h
Coaster Holder Size: 5"w x 5"h x 2½"d
Instructions: Follow charts and use required stitches to work Hummingbird Coaster Set pieces. Use antique white for all joining. Join long unworked edges of Top Sides to Top. Join Top Sides along short edges. For Bottom, cut a piece of plastic canvas 32 x 32 threads. **(Note:** Bottom is not worked.) Join long unworked edges of Bottom Sides to Bottom. Join Bottom Sides along short edges. For Coaster backing, cut cork or felt slightly smaller than Coaster. Glue cork or felt to wrong side of stitched piece.

HUMMINGBIRD MAGNETS

Size: 5¼"w x 4"h each
Instructions: Follow charts and use required stitches to work Magnets. Glue magnetic strip to wrong side of each stitched piece.

HUMMINGBIRD BOOKEND

Size: 8⅜"w x 4¼"h x 2¾"d
(Note: Fits a 8"w x 3⅝"h x 2⅛"d brick.)
Instructions: Follow charts and use required stitches to work Bookend pieces. Use antique white for all joining. Join Long Sides to Short Sides along short edges. Join Front to Long Sides and Short Sides. Wrap brick in plastic wrap and insert brick into Bookend. Join Back to Long Sides and Short Sides.

"GOD BLESS OUR NEST" SIGN

Size: 11⅝"w x 7¼"h
Instructions: Follow chart and use required stitches to work "God Bless Our Nest" Sign. Use sewing needle and thread to attach sawtooth hanger to wrong side of stitched piece.

Hummingbird designs by Kathleen Hurley.
"God Bless Our Nest" Sign border design by Virginia Hockenbury.

NL	COLOR		NL	COLOR
00	black - 2 yds		29	dk blue green - 26 yds
03	burgundy - 9 yds		36	blue - 25 yds
14	brown - 14 yds		39	ecru - 35 yds
16	beige - 17 yds		41	antique white - 183 yds
24	green - 4 yds		42	lt burgundy - 12 yds
25	lt green - 3 yds		53	blue green - 25 yds

Coaster Holder Bottom Side (32 x 16 threads) (Work 4)

Coaster Holder Top (34 x 34 threads)

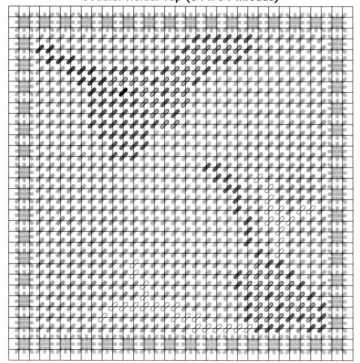

Coaster Holder Top Side (34 x 6 threads) (Work 4)

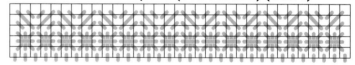

Coaster (30 x 30 threads) (Work 8)

37

NL	COLOR	NL	COLOR	NL	COLOR
00	black	24	green	39	ecru
03	burgundy	25	lt green	41	antique white
14	brown	29	dk blue green	42	lt burgundy
16	beige	36	blue	53	blue green

Magnet A (35 x 26 threads)

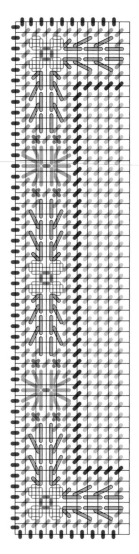

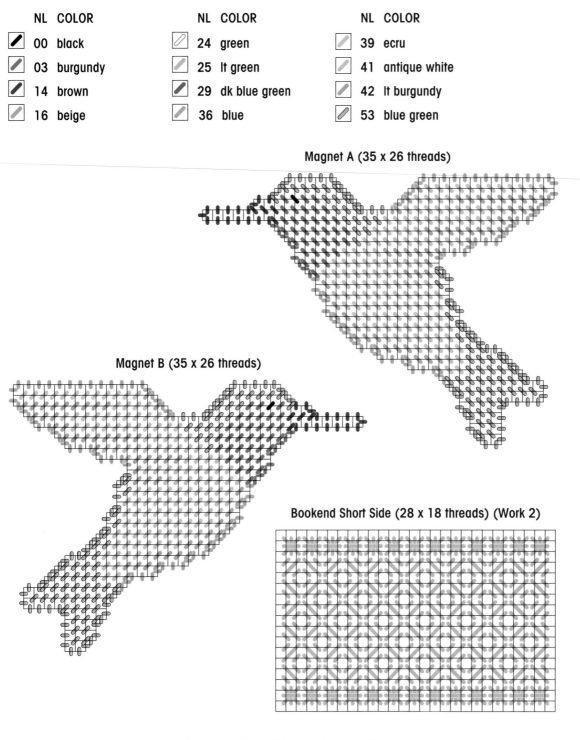

Magnet B (35 x 26 threads)

Bookend Short Side (28 x 18 threads) (Work 2)

Bookend Long Side (56 x 18 threads) (Work 2)

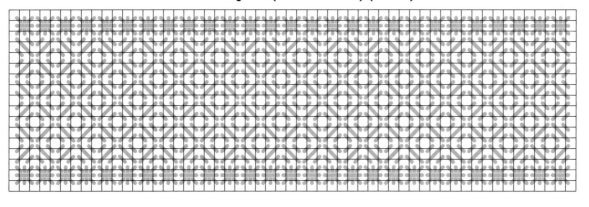

"God Bless Our Nest" Sign (78 x 49 threads)

Bookend Front/Back (56 x 28 threads) (Work 2)

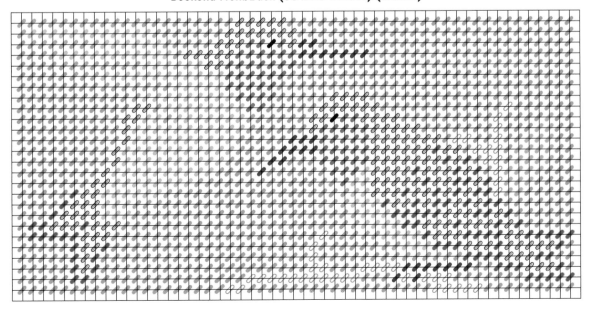

SPRING HOUSE

Skill Level: Advanced

Size With Base: 8½"w x 5"h x 8½"d

Supplies: Worsted weight yarn or Needloft® Plastic Canvas Yarn (refer to color keys), DMC embroidery floss (refer to color keys), three 10½" x 13½" sheets of 7 mesh plastic canvas, one 10½" x 13½" sheet of 10 mesh plastic canvas, one 8" x 11" sheet of 14 mesh plastic canvas, two 4mm round gold beads, #16 tapestry needle, #20 tapestry needle, #24 tapestry needle, and clear-drying craft glue

Stitches Used: Backstitch, French Knot, Gobelin Stitch, Mosaic Stitch, Overcast Stitch, and Tent Stitch

Instructions: Photo model was stitched using worsted weight yarn and embroidery floss. Cut Shrub and Tree pieces from 10 mesh plastic canvas. Cut Flower Stems and Flower Petals from 14 mesh plastic canvas. Cut remaining pieces from 7 mesh plastic canvas.

Work Base through two thicknesses of canvas. Leaving stitches in shaded areas unworked, follow charts and use required stitches to work remaining Spring House pieces. Use 12 strands of embroidery floss to work 10 mesh plastic canvas pieces. Use 6 strands of embroidery floss to work 14 mesh plastic canvas pieces. Use 6 strands of embroidery floss to work Backstitch vines and French Knot flowers on Fence pieces.

Refer to Diagram and photos for assembly. Use white to join House Front to House Sides. Use white and match ▲'s to join Back Wall to House Sides. Use white to join House Back to House Sides. Use pink to join Roof Front to Roof Back along unworked edges. Use pink to join Extension Roof pieces along unworked edges. Use grey to join long unworked edges of Chimney Sides to Chimney Front. Use grey to join remaining unworked edges of Chimney Sides to Chimney Back.

For each long fence section, place wrong sides of two Fence C pieces together. With edges even, work stitches in shaded area through two thicknesses to join Fence C pieces together. Use white to join Fence C pieces along remaining unworked edges. Repeat for two remaining long fence sections. For each short fence section, place wrong side of one Fence A piece and wrong side of one Fence B piece together. Work stitches in shaded areas through two thicknesses to join short ends of Fence A and Fence B together. Use white to join Fence A and Fence B along remaining unworked edges. Repeat for remaining short fence section.

Use white and match ◆'s and ✚'s to tack House to Base. Use white, match like symbols, and refer to photos to tack fence sections to Base. Use white to tack fence sections together.

Refer to photo for placement and glue Roof to House Sides. Glue Extension Roof to Back Wall and House Back. Glue Chimney to Roof. Glue Large Shutters to House Front. Glue Small Shutters to House Back. Glue Tree A pieces to Tree B pieces. Glue Shrub A pieces to Shrub B pieces. Glue Flower Petals to Flower Stems. Glue Trees to House Sides. Glue Shrubs to House Front. Glue Flowers to House Front and House Back. Glue one bead to each door.

Chimney Back (5 x 4 threads)

Chimney Front (5 x 7 threads)

Chimney Side A (5 x 7 threads)

Chimney Side B (5 x 7 threads)

House Front (24 x 21 threads)

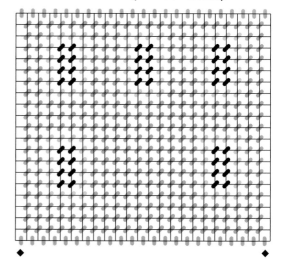

NL	COLOR		DMC	COLOR
32	blue - 5 yds		962	pink embroidery floss - 18 yds
37	grey - 7 yds		975	brown embroidery floss - 3 yds
38	dk grey - 4 yds		992	lt green embroidery floss - 40 yds
41	white - 73 yds		3814	green embroidery floss - 11 yds
55	pink - 16 yds			

House Back (24 x 23 threads)

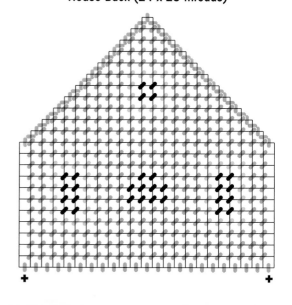

Back Wall (24 x 10 threads)

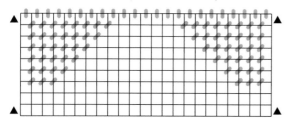

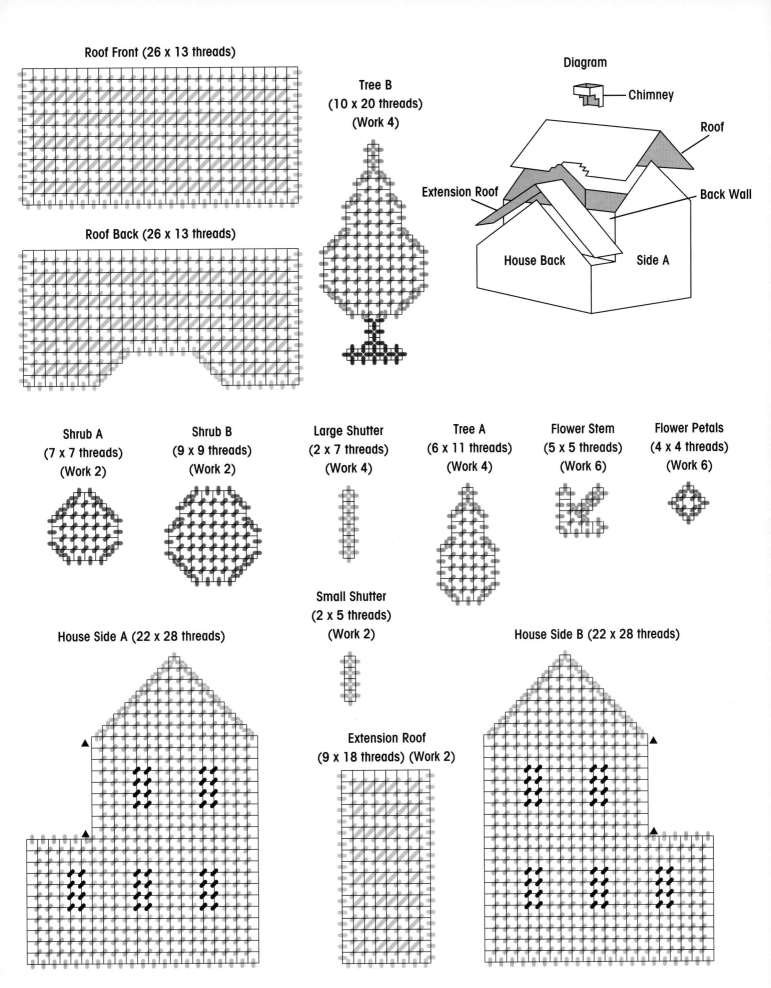

Roof Front (26 x 13 threads)

Roof Back (26 x 13 threads)

Tree B
(10 x 20 threads)
(Work 4)

Diagram

Chimney

Roof

Extension Roof

Back Wall

House Back

Side A

Shrub A
(7 x 7 threads)
(Work 2)

Shrub B
(9 x 9 threads)
(Work 2)

Large Shutter
(2 x 7 threads)
(Work 4)

Tree A
(6 x 11 threads)
(Work 4)

Flower Stem
(5 x 5 threads)
(Work 6)

Flower Petals
(4 x 4 threads)
(Work 6)

Small Shutter
(2 x 5 threads)
(Work 2)

House Side A (22 x 28 threads)

House Side B (22 x 28 threads)

Extension Roof
(9 x 18 threads) (Work 2)

NL	COLOR		DMC	COLOR
	37 grey		992	lt green embroidery floss
41 white			962	pink embroidery floss Fr. Knot
53 green - 40 yds				

Fence A (17 x 9 threads) (Work 2)

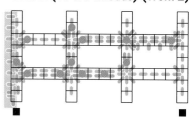

Fence B (17 x 9 threads) (Work 2)

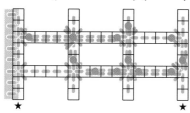

Fence C (42 x 9 threads) (Work 6)

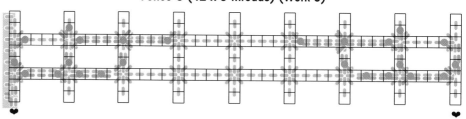

Base (56 x 56 threads) (Cut 2)

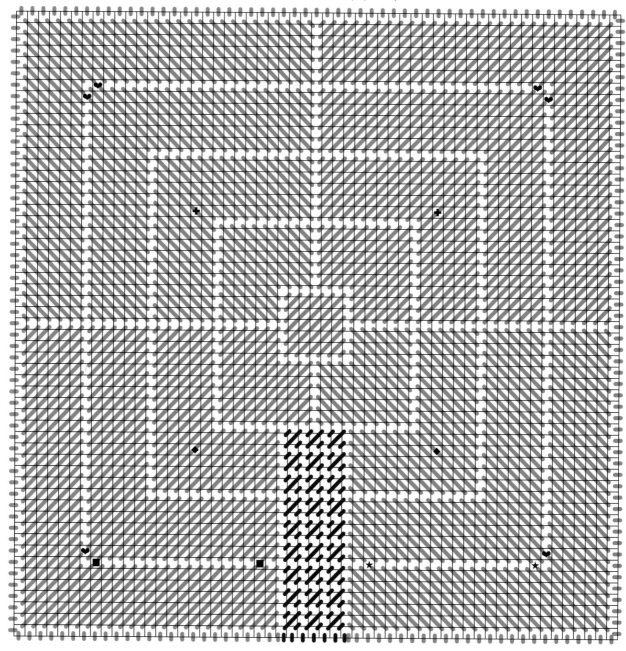

ROSE MOTIF CENTERPIECE
Skill Level: Intermediate
Size: 5"w x 5⅝"h x 5"d
Supplies: Worsted weight yarn or Needloft® Plastic Canvas Yarn (refer to color key), one 10½" x 13½" sheet of 7 mesh plastic canvas, one Uniek® 5" hexagon shape, and #16 tapestry needle
Stitches Used: Backstitch, Cross Stitch, Gobelin Stitch, Overcast Stitch, Rose Stitch, Six-Trip Herringbone Stitch, and Tent Stitch
Instructions: Photo model was stitched using worsted weight yarn. Follow charts and use required stitches to work Sides, leaving stitches in shaded areas unworked. Use white to join Sides between ■'s. Work stitches in shaded areas, continuing the Six-Trip Herringbone Stitch around Centerpiece. For Base, trim hanger from 5" hexagon shape. (**Note:** Base is not worked.) Use white to join Sides to Base.

Side (19 x 34 threads) (Work 6)

NL	COLOR	NL	COLOR
✎ 03	dk pink - 14 yds	✎ 26	green - 3 yds
✎ 05	pink - 14 yds	✎ 41	white - 30 yds
✎ 07	lt pink - 7 yds		

LAMB BASKET
Skill Level: Beginner
Size: 4¼"w x 3¼"h x 2⅜"d
Supplies: Worsted weight yarn or Needloft® Plastic Canvas Yarn (refer to color key), one 10½" x 13½" sheet of 7 mesh plastic canvas, and #16 tapestry needle
Stitches Used: French Knot, Gobelin Stitch, Overcast Stitch, Tent Stitch, and Turkey Loop Stitch
Instructions: Photo model was stitched using worsted weight yarn. Follow charts and use required stitches to work Lamb Basket pieces, leaving stitches in shaded areas unworked. For Bottom and Sides, cut three pieces of plastic canvas 12 x 18 threads each. Use green Gobelin Stitches over two threads to cover Bottom and Sides. Work stitches in shaded areas to join Front and Back to long edges of Sides. Use color to match closest stitching area to join Bottom to Sides, Front, and Back. Work green Overcast Stitches to cover unworked edges. Refer to photo for placement and glue Flowers and Ears to Front and Back.

NL	COLOR
✎ 00	black
✎ 07	pink
✎ 23	green
✎ 41	white
● 00	black Fr. Knot
● 57	yellow Fr. Knot
○ 23	green Turkey Loop

Lamb Basket design by Dick Martin.

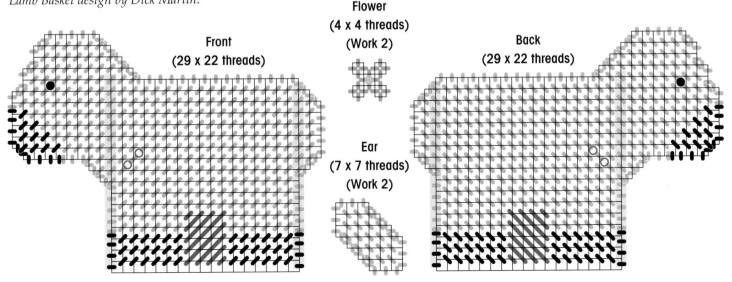

Front (29 x 22 threads)

Flower (4 x 4 threads) (Work 2)

Ear (7 x 7 threads) (Work 2)

Back (29 x 22 threads)

MINIATURE BASKETS

(**Note:** Photo models were stitched using worsted weight yarn.)

Skill Level: Beginner

Supplies For All Three Baskets: Worsted weight yarn or Needloft® Plastic Canvas Yarn (refer to color key), one 10½" x 13½" sheet of 7 mesh plastic canvas, one 3" dia plastic canvas circle, one 4" dia plastic canvas circle, and #16 tapestry needle

Stitches Used: Alicia Lace, Fern Stitch, Gobelin Stitch, Overcast Stitch, and Tent Stitch

HAT BASKET

Size: 2½"w x 3½"h x 3"d

Instructions: For Rim and Bottom, refer to charts to cut the 3" dia plastic canvas circle. Use the five outer threads for Rim. Use the four inner threads for Bottom. Follow charts and use required stitches to work Hat Basket pieces. Use tan for all joining and tacking. With wrong side facing inward, match ■'s to join short edges of Side, forming a cylinder. Join Bottom to Side. Join inner edge of Rim to remaining unworked edge of Side. Match ◆'s to tack Handle to Side.

MAY BASKET

Size: 3½"w x 3"h x 3¾"d

Instructions: Follow charts and use required stitches to work May Basket pieces. Use tan for all joining. Match ▲'s and place wrong sides of Top and Bottom together. Join Top and Bottom along all edges. With wrong side facing inward, join unworked edges of Handle to Top and Bottom at ▲'s.

FLOWER BASKET

Size: 2½"w x 2½"h x 2¼"d

Instructions: For Bottom, keep outer threads intact and cut three threads from center of the 4" dia plastic canvas circle. For Side, trim two inner threads from the remaining section of the 4" dia circle. Refer to chart to cut remaining section in half. Follow charts and use required stitches to work Flower Basket pieces. Use tan for all joining and tacking. With wrong side facing inward, match ★'s to join Side along straight edges, forming a funnel. Join Bottom to small end of Side. With wrong side facing inward, match ✳'s to tack Handle to Side.

Hat Basket design by Catherine Bihlmaier.

NL COLOR

Hat Basket Bottom

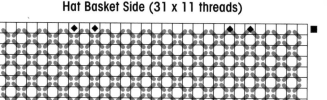

Hat Basket Side (31 x 11 threads)

Hat Basket Handle (37 x 4 threads)

Hat Basket Rim

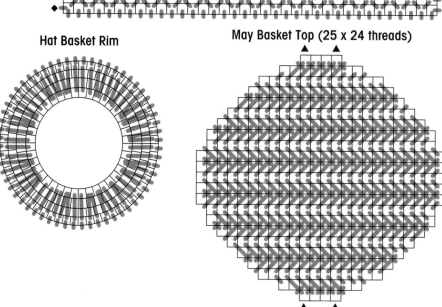

May Basket Top (25 x 24 threads)

May Basket Handle (41 x 5 threads)

Flower Basket Bottom

May Basket Bottom (25 x 27 threads)

Flower Basket Side

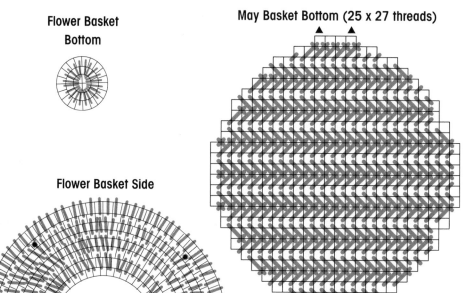

Flower Basket Handle (28 x 2 threads)

	NL	COLOR
▨	18	tan

EASTER BUNNY
DOOR DECORATION
Skill Level: Intermediate
Size: 14½"w x 17¾"h x 1¼"d
Supplies: Worsted weight yarn or Needloft® Plastic Canvas Yarn (refer to color keys), three 10½" x 13½" sheets of 7 mesh plastic canvas, two 1" lengths of black cloth-covered floral wire, sawtooth hanger, sewing needle and thread, #16 tapestry needle, and clear-drying craft glue
Stitches Used: Backstitch, Cross Stitch, French Knot, Gobelin Stitch, Mosaic Stitch, Overcast Stitch, and Tent Stitch
Instructions: Photo model was stitched using worsted weight yarn. Follow charts and use required stitches to work Easter Bunny Door Decoration pieces, leaving stitches in shaded areas unworked. Match ■'s and ◗'s and work stitches in shaded areas of Bunny to join Ear A and Ear B to wrong side of Bunny. Match ▲'s to place Hat Brim on Bunny. Work tan Overcast Stitches along unworked edges of Hat Brim to join Hat Brim to Bunny and Ears. Use white and match ★'s and ♣'s to join long unworked edges of Bow Tie to Bunny. Using white, match ♦'s and work through three thicknesses to join unworked edges of Bow Tie Center to Bow Tie and Bunny. Refer to photo for placement and use color to match closest stitching area to tack Leaves and Flowers to Bunny and Hat Brim. For bow, cut a 12" length of aqua yarn. Tie yarn in a bow. Use aqua to tack bow to Bunny. Tack bow ends to Bunny. Trim bow ends. For antennas, refer to photo for placement and glue shaped wires to wrong side of Butterfly. Use lt gold to tack Butterfly to Bunny. Use sewing needle and thread to attach sawtooth hanger to wrong side of Bunny.

Easter Bunny Door Decoration design by Dick Martin.

NL	COLOR
08	lt pink
21	yellow

Ear A (31 x 53 threads)

Ear B (31 x 53 threads)

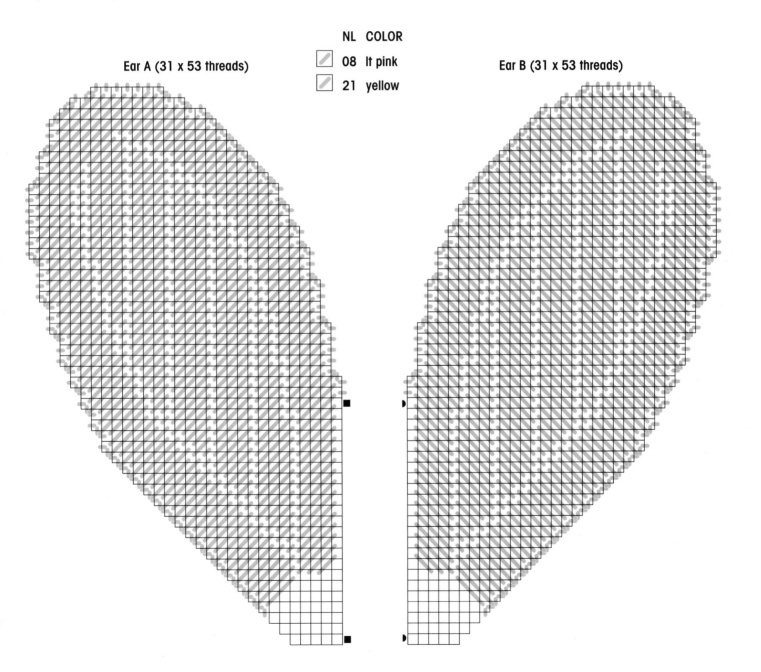

NL	COLOR		NL	COLOR
 00	black - 3 yds		41	white - 28 yds
07	pink - 6 yds		43	tan - 35 yds
08	lt pink - 28 yds		45	lavender - 4 yds
11	gold - 4 yds		47	peach - 1 yd
12	orange -2 yds		49	aqua - 21 yds
21	yellow - 120 yds		07	pink Fr. Knot
24	dk green - 3 yds		11	gold Fr. Knot
25	green - 4 yds		45	lavender Fr. Knot
39	lt gold - 2 yds			

Medium Flower (10 x 10 threads)

Small Flower (6 x 6 threads)

Large Flower (14 x 14 threads)

Butterfly (12 x 10 threads)

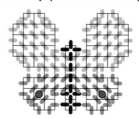

Bow Tie (48 x 18 threads)

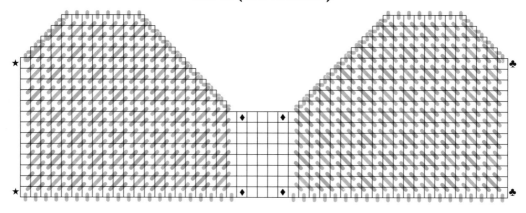

Leaf A (16 x 10 threads)

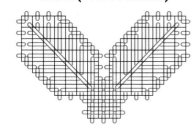

Bow Tie Center (6 x 10 threads)

Leaf B (16 x 10 threads)

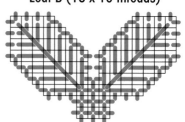

Hat Brim (68 x 15 threads)

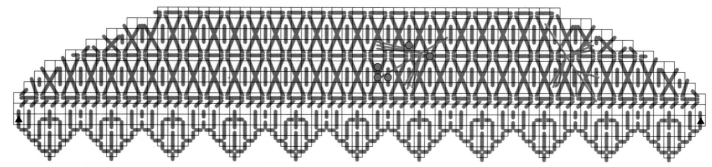

Bunny (70 x 88 threads)

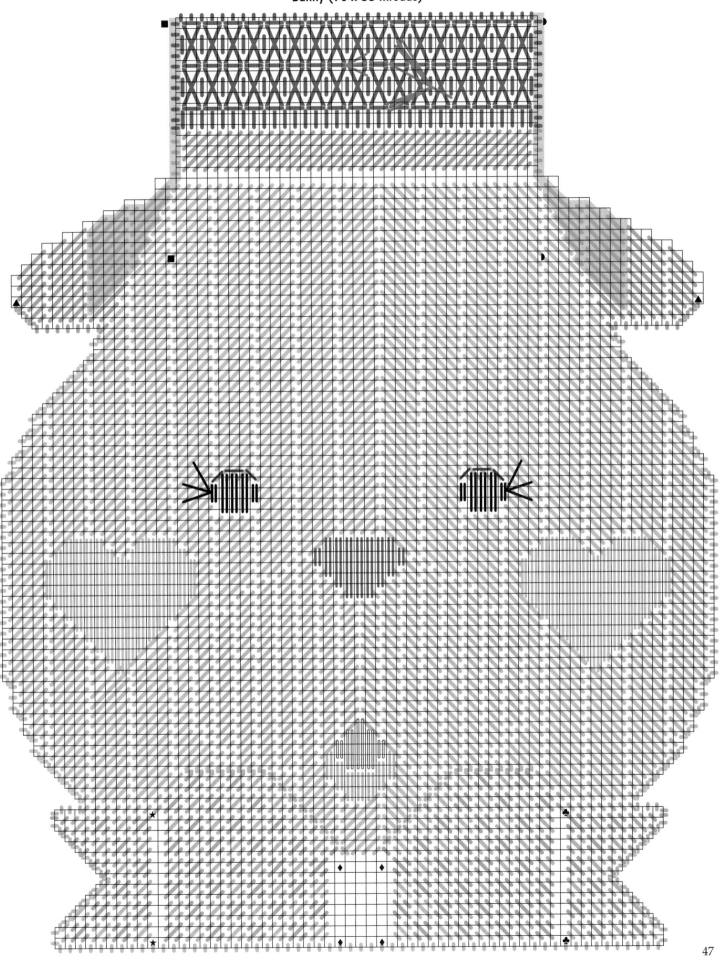

SUMMER

With their bright golden petals resembling the rays of the sun, it's no wonder that sunflowers are favorite summer blooms. The giant flowers are perfect for preserving on canvas. A gardenful of sunflowers reaches toward the sky on our wall hanging and tissue box cover, and the coordinating quilt-block magnet reflects the sunny shades of summer. All the fun and excitement of the season, including a star-spangled Independence Day, is captured in this "sun-sational" collection!

Images of country life are reflected in the lighthearted projects on these pages. Our colorful tissue box cover (below) captures the charm of an old red barn. Its doors and windows open to reveal a host of country characters! (Opposite) Dressed in a jaunty bow tie, our fun-loving frog stick-up (top left) will make a big "splash" when displayed in your window. Fashioned in black and white, our whimsical wind sock (top right) resembles a Holstein cow. A miniature bell around her neck jingles when she's caught by a breeze! A honeybee magnet (bottom) adds a sweet touch to your kitchen, especially when it's paired with our bright floral magnet. And our bovine magnet is sure to remind you to drink your milk!

A single butterfly dancing in the breeze can lure us outdoors during the sunny days of summer. Stitched on 14 mesh canvas with embroidery floss, our butterfly plant poke (right) is perfect for adding a bright touch to a houseplant. A three-dimensional magnolia blossom (below) adorns a simple piece of driftwood to create a stunning accent. For those whose tastes run to the Southwest, our coaster set (opposite, top) features three varieties of cacti: barrel, prickly pear, and saguaro. Trimmed with a seashell border, our market-style basket (opposite, bottom) makes a pretty — and useful — addition to the bath.

Our watermelon and canning jar magnets (right) preserve a gardenful of summertime crops. The colorful motifs are also arranged on a grapevine wreath (opposite) with silk greenery and miniature baskets. Reflecting images of the season, our jar lids are great for topping jars filled with summer treats and collectibles. Created with 7 mesh plastic canvas shapes, our all-American trinket box (below) will fill your home with patriotic spirit for the Fourth of July.

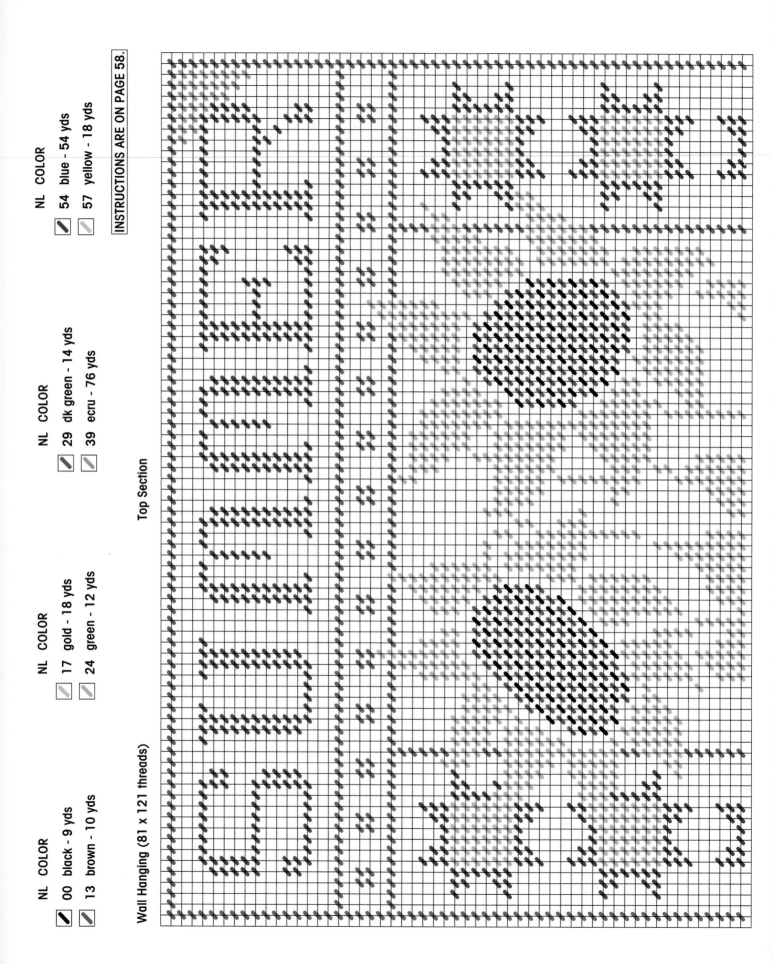

NL COLOR

☑ 00 black - 9 yds

☑ 13 brown - 10 yds

NL COLOR

☑ 17 gold - 18 yds

☑ 24 green - 12 yds

NL COLOR

☑ 29 dk green - 14 yds

☑ 39 ecru - 76 yds

NL COLOR

☑ 54 blue - 54 yds

☑ 57 yellow - 18 yds

INSTRUCTIONS ARE ON PAGE 58.

Top Section

Wall Hanging (81 x 121 threads)

56

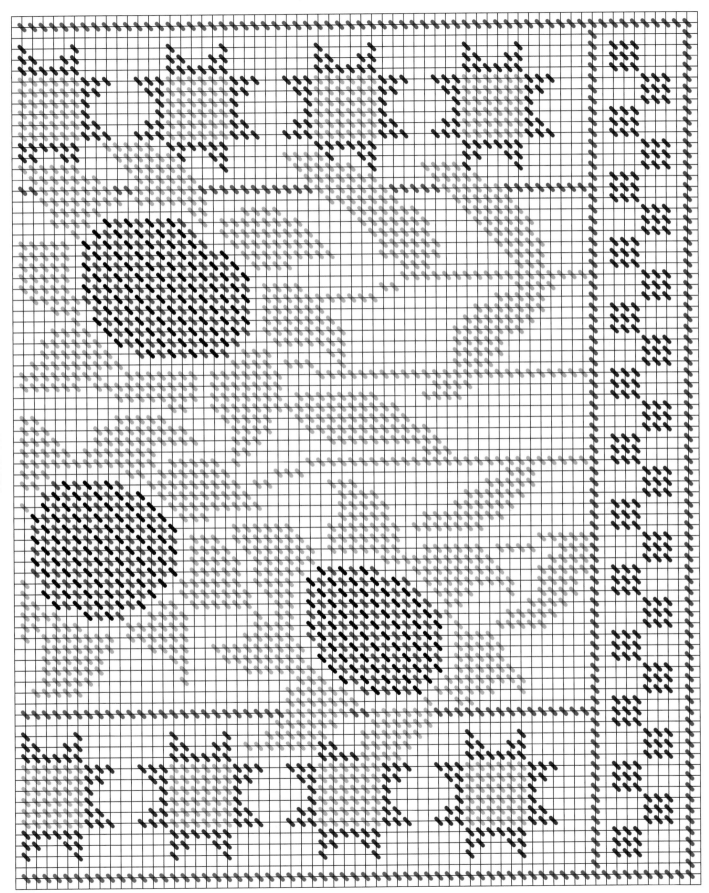

SUMMER WALL HANGING

Skill Level: Intermediate
Size: 12"w x 18"h
Supplies: Needloft® Plastic Canvas Yarn or worsted weight yarn (refer to color key), one 12" x 18" sheet of 7 mesh plastic canvas, #16 tapestry needle, sewing needle and thread, and sawtooth hanger
Stitches Used: Overcast Stitch and Tent Stitch
Instructions: Photo model was stitched using Needloft® Plastic Canvas Yarn. (**Note:** Design fits a 12" x 18" sheet of canvas.) Follow chart and use required stitches to work Top Section. Follow chart and use required stitches to work Bottom Section below Top Section. Complete background with ecru Tent Stitches as indicated on chart. Use ecru Overcast Stitches to cover unworked edges. Use sewing needle and thread to attach sawtooth hanger to wrong side of stitched piece.

SUMMER TISSUE BOX COVER

Skill Level: Beginner
Size: 4½"w x 5¾"h x 4½"d
(**Note:** Fits a 4¼"w x 5¼"h x 4¼"d boutique tissue box.)
Supplies: Needloft® Plastic Canvas Yarn or worsted weight yarn (refer to color key), one 10½" x 13½" sheet of 7 mesh plastic canvas, and #16 tapestry needle
Stitches Used: Overcast Stitch and Tent Stitch
Instructions: Photo model was stitched using Needloft® Plastic Canvas Yarn. Follow charts and use required stitches to work Tissue Box Cover pieces. Complete backgrounds with ecru Tent Stitches as indicated on charts. Use blue for all joining. Join Sides along long edges. Join Top to Sides.

SUMMER MAGNET

Skill Level: Beginner
Size: 2"w x 2"h
Supplies: Needloft® Plastic Canvas Yarn or worsted weight yarn (refer to color key), one 10½" x 13½" sheet of 7 mesh plastic canvas, #16 tapestry needle, magnetic strip, and clear-drying craft glue
Stitches Used: Overcast Stitch and Tent Stitch
Instructions: Photo model was stitched using Needloft® Plastic Canvas Yarn. Follow chart and use required stitches to work Magnet. Glue magnetic strip to wrong side of stitched piece.

Summer Set designs by Polly Carbonari.

NL	COLOR	
00	black - 4 yds	
13	brown - 4 yds	
17	gold - 8 yds	
24	green - 13 yds	
39	ecru - 52 yds	
54	blue - 11 yds	
57	yellow - 8 yds	

Magnet (14 x 14 threads)

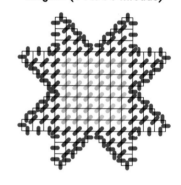

Tissue Box Cover Side (30 x 38 threads) (Work 4)

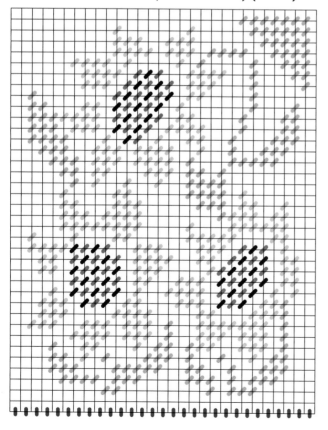

Tissue Box Cover Top (30 x 30 threads)

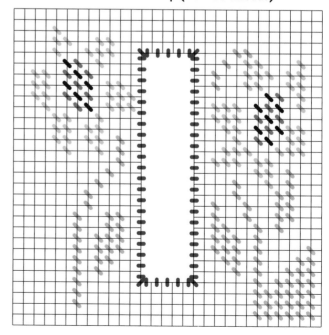

FROG STICK-UP

Skill Level: Beginner

Size: 6¾"w x 5½"h x 1"d

Supplies: Worsted weight yarn or Needloft® Plastic Canvas Yarn (refer to color key), one 10½" x 13½" sheet of 7 mesh plastic canvas, #16 tapestry needle, two 14mm moving eyes, two 20mm suction cups, two 1" dia green pom-poms, 3" of black cloth-covered floral wire, and clear-drying craft glue

Stitches Used: Backstitch, Bullion Knot, Cross Stitch, French Knot, Overcast Stitch, and Tent Stitch

Instructions: Photo model was stitched using worsted weight yarn. Follow charts and use required stitches to work Frog Stick-Up pieces. Use orange to work Bullion Knot on Front between 1 and 2. Refer to photo for placement to insert and glue suction cups into openings on Front. With wrong sides together, use green to join Front to Back. For Mouth, refer to photo to shape and glue floral wire to Front. Glue eyes and Tie to Front. For Feet, glue pom-poms to Front at ▲'s. Glue Feet to pom-poms.

Frog Stick-Up design by Sandy and Honey for Studio M.

NL	COLOR		NL	COLOR
27	green - 43 yds		57	yellow Fr. Knot
57	yellow - 6 yds		58	orange Fr. Knot
58	orange - 3 yds			

Front (45 x 35 threads)

Tie (18 x 9 threads)

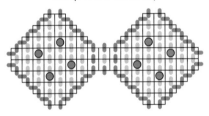

Right Foot (17 x 14 threads)

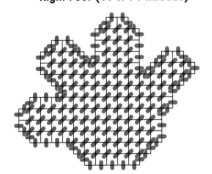

Left Foot (17 x 14 threads)

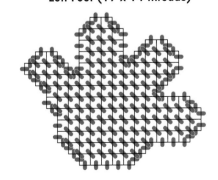

Back (45 x 35 threads)

COW WIND SOCK

Skill Level: Beginner
Size: 4½"h x 3" dia

Supplies: Worsted weight yarn or Needloft® Plastic Canvas Yarn (refer to color key), one 10½" x 13½" sheet of 7 mesh plastic canvas, #16 tapestry needle, two 10mm moving eyes, ½" copper cowbell, twelve 15" lengths of ¼"w white satin ribbon, one 11" length of ¼"w white satin ribbon, four 15" lengths of ¼"w black satin ribbon, one 8" length of ¼"w black satin ribbon, and clear-drying craft glue

Stitches Used: Backstitch, Cross Stitch, Fringe, Gobelin Stitch, Overcast Stitch, Tent Stitch, and Turkey Loop Stitch

Instructions: Photo model was stitched using worsted weight yarn. Follow charts and use required stitches to work Cow Wind Sock pieces, leaving shaded areas unworked. Match ▲'s and work stitches in shaded areas through two thicknesses to join short edges of Wind Sock, forming a cylinder. Glue one 15" length of black ribbon to wrong side of Wind Sock at each ★. Glue three 15" lengths of white ribbon to wrong side of Wind Sock between the black ribbons.

For hanger, refer to photo for placement and glue remaining 11" length of white ribbon to wrong side of Wind Sock. Use black yarn to tack Ears to Wind Sock. Use white yarn and match ✳'s to tack Tail to Wind Sock. Use white yarn to tack cowbell to Wind Sock. Glue eyes to Wind Sock. Tie remaining black ribbon into a bow and trim ends. Glue to Wind Sock and cowbell.

Cow Wind Sock design by Lori Turner.

NL	COLOR	
✏	00	black - 5 yds
✏	07	pink - 1 yd
✏	41	white - 39 yds
◎	00	black Fringe
◎	41	white Fringe
◎	41	white Turkey Loop

Tail
(3 x 12 threads)

Ear A
(6 x 4 threads)

Ear B
(6 x 4 threads)

Wind Sock (64 x 31 threads)

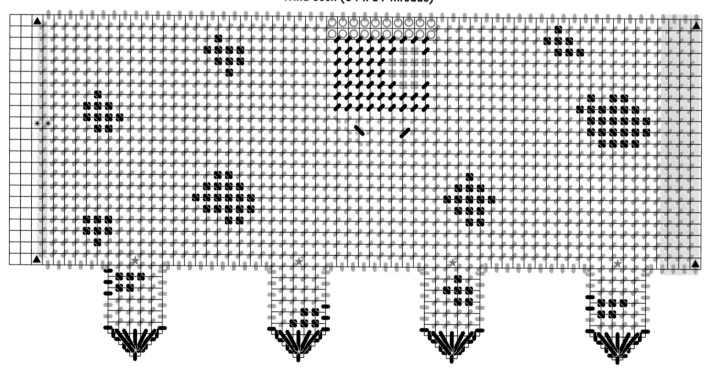

VARIETY MAGNETS

Skill Level: Beginner

Approx Size: 3¾"w x 3⅜"h each

Supplies: Worsted weight yarn or Needloft® Plastic Canvas Yarn (refer to color key), one 10½" x 13½" sheet of 7 mesh plastic canvas, #16 tapestry needle, two 8mm moving eyes, two 10mm moving eyes, 6" of black cloth-covered floral wire, magnetic strip, and clear-drying craft glue

Stitches Used: Backstitch, Bullion Knot, Cross Stitch, Fringe, Overcast Stitch, and Tent Stitch

Instructions: Photo models were stitched using worsted weight yarn. Follow charts and use required stitches to work Magnet pieces. Glue magnetic strip to wrong side of completed stitched piece. **For Cow only,** refer to photo for placement and glue 10mm eyes to Cow. **For Bee only,** use orange to work Bullion Knot on Bee Body between **1** and **2**. Refer to photo for placement and glue Bee Wings to wrong side of Bee Body. Cut floral wire into three 2" lengths. Refer to photo to shape and glue floral wire to Bee. Glue 8mm eyes to Bee Body. **For Rose only,** use red for all joining. With right side curved inward, join unworked edges of Petal A together. Repeat for remaining Petal A pieces. With right side curved inward, match ★'s to join unworked edges of Petal B together. Repeat for remaining Petal B pieces. Refer to photo for placement and glue Petal B pieces together. Refer to photo for placement and glue Petal A pieces to Petal B pieces. Glue Petals to Rose Base. Glue Rose Base to Leaves.

Cow Magnet design by Beth Siegal.
Bee and Rose Magnet designs by Sandy and Honey for Studio M

NL	COLOR
✎ 00	black
✎ 02	red
✎ 07	pink
✎ 16	tan
✎ 23	dk green
✎ 25	green
✎ 41	white
✎ 57	yellow
✎ 58	orange
○ 57	yellow Fringe

Petal A
(8 x 8 threads)
(Work 3)

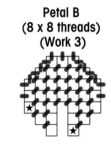

Petal B
(8 x 8 threads)
(Work 3)

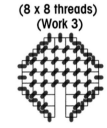

Rose Base (18 x 18 threads)

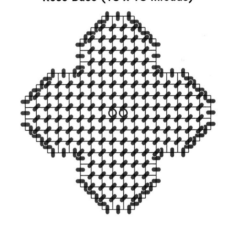

Leaves (29 x 9 threads)

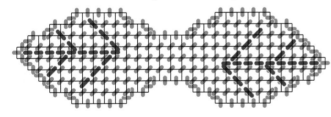

Bee Wings (21 x 21 threads)

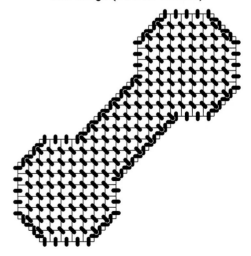

Cow (20 x 20 threads)

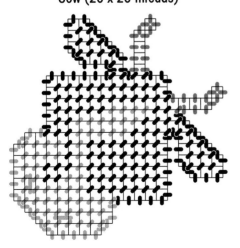

Bee Body (19 x 19 threads)

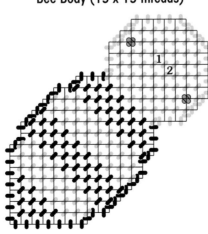

RED BARN TISSUE BOX COVER

Skill Level: Beginner

Size: 5"w x 6⅞"h x 5¾"d

(**Note:** Fits a 4¼"w x 5¼"h x 4¼"d boutique tissue box.)

Supplies: Worsted weight yarn or Needloft® Plastic Canvas Yarn (refer to color key), metallic silver cord, three 10½" x 13½" sheets of 7 mesh plastic canvas, #16 tapestry needle, ⅛"w pink satin ribbon, and clear-drying craft glue

Stitches Used: Backstitch, Cross Stitch, French Knot, Gobelin Stitch, Overcast Stitch, Scotch Stitch, Tent Stitch, and Turkey Loop Stitch

Instructions: Photo model was stitched using worsted weight yarn. Follow charts and use required stitches to work Red Barn Tissue Box Cover pieces.

Refer to photo for placement and use white to join Front and Back to Sides. Use black to join one Roof Side to one Roof Top along one long edge. Repeat for remaining Roof pieces. Use black to join Roof Top pieces together. Use black to join Roof to Front, Back, and Sides. Use white to join two Shutter B pieces to Front. Use white to join Door C to Front. Use white to join Door B pieces to Front. Use white Overcast Stitches to cover unworked edge of Door B piece. Use black to tack Cow to Front. Use white to join Door A pieces to Side A. Use white Overcast Stitches to cover unworked edge of Door A piece. Use white to join two Shutter A pieces to Side A. Use white to join two Shutter B pieces to Back. Use white to join four Shutter A pieces to Side B. Tie ribbon in a bow and trim ends. Glue ribbon to Side B.

Red Barn Tissue Box Cover design by Peggy Astle.

NL	COLOR		NL	COLOR		NL	COLOR		NL	COLOR
00	black - 27 yds		14	brown - 4 yds		33	blue - 2 yds			red Fr. Knot*
	black*			brown*		41	white - 33 yds		00	black Turkey Loop
02	red - 65 yds		16	lt brown - 3 yds		56	flesh - 3 yds		14	brown Turkey Loop
05	pink - 2 yds		17	gold - 2 yds			metallic silver cord - 2 yds			
07	lt pink - 2 yds		27	green - 4 yds			black Fr. Knot*			

* Use 2-ply yarn.

Front (31 x 45 threads)

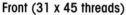
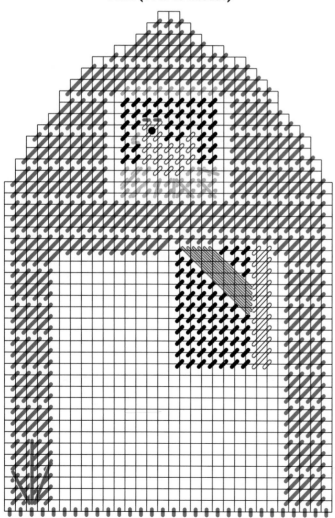

Back (31 x 45 threads)

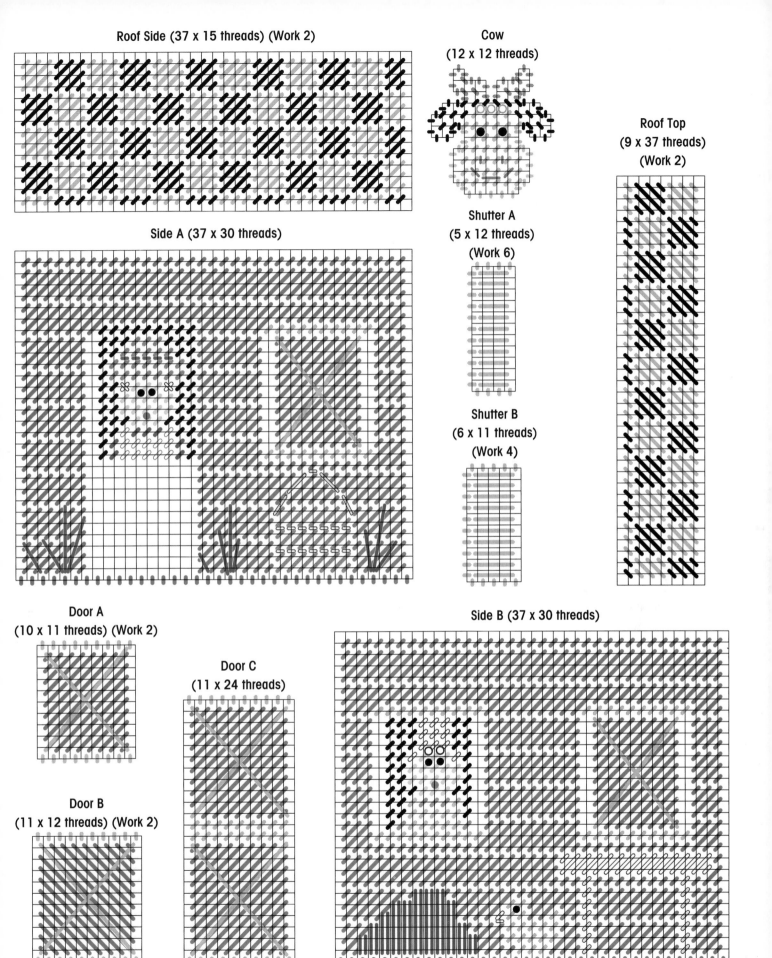

Roof Side (37 x 15 threads) (Work 2)

Cow
(12 x 12 threads)

Roof Top
(9 x 37 threads)
(Work 2)

Side A (37 x 30 threads)

Shutter A
(5 x 12 threads)
(Work 6)

Shutter B
(6 x 11 threads)
(Work 4)

Door A
(10 x 11 threads) (Work 2)

Door C
(11 x 24 threads)

Door B
(11 x 12 threads) (Work 2)

Side B (37 x 30 threads)

BUTTERFLY PLANT POKE

Skill Level: Intermediate
Size: 2¾"w x 2"h
Supplies: DMC embroidery floss (refer to color key), one 8" x 11" sheet of 14 mesh plastic canvas, #24 tapestry needle, one 3" piece of black cloth-covered floral wire, wooden skewer, and clear-drying craft glue
Stitches Used: Cross Stitch, Gobelin Stitch, Overcast Stitch, and Tent Stitch
Instructions: Photo model was stitched using DMC embroidery floss. Use three strands of embroidery floss for all stitches. Follow charts and use required stitches to work Butterfly pieces. Use six strands of brown embroidery floss to join Wing A to Wing B along unworked edges. Cut floral wire into 1½" pieces. Refer to photo for placement and glue shaped wire to wrong side of Butterfly. Glue wooden skewer to wrong side of Butterfly.

Butterfly Plant Poke design by Jack Peatman for LuvLee Designs.

DMC COLOR

✎	352	peach
✎	353	lt peach
✎	898	brown

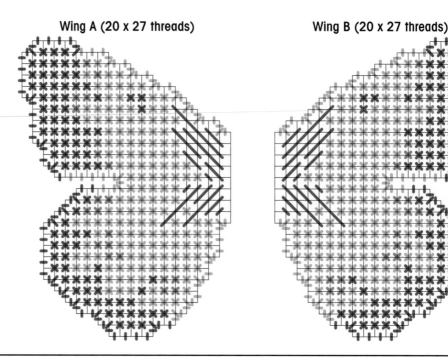

Wing A (20 x 27 threads)   **Wing B (20 x 27 threads)**

MAGNOLIA CENTERPIECE

Skill Level: Intermediate
Design Size: 7½"w x 8½"h
Supplies: Worsted weight yarn or Needloft® Plastic Canvas Yarn (refer to color key), two 10½" x 13½" sheets of 7 mesh plastic canvas, #16 tapestry needle, one piece of driftwood, and clear-drying craft glue
Stitches Used: Gobelin Stitch, Overcast Stitch, and Tent Stitch
Instructions: Photo model was stitched using worsted weight yarn. Follow charts to work Magnolia Centerpiece pieces. Use ecru to join one Left Petal to one Right Petal along unworked edges. Repeat for remaining Petal pieces. Use brown to join Center pieces along unworked edges.
Refer to photo for placement and glue Leaves to driftwood. Glue Petals to Leaves and driftwood. Glue Center to Petals.

Magnolia Centerpiece design by Kenneth Cormier.

NL COLOR

✎	15	brown - 1 yd
✎	29	green - 20 yds
✎	39	ecru - 25 yds

Left Petal   **Right Petal**
(8 x 19 threads)   **(8 x 19 threads)**
(Work 8)   **(Work 8)**

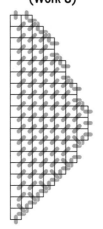

Center
(5 x 5 threads)
(Work 3)

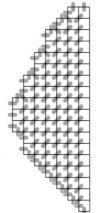

Leaf (33 x 14 threads) (Work 4)

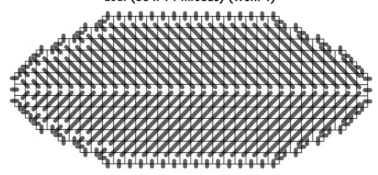

SEASHELL BASKET

Skill Level: Intermediate

Size: 9½"w x 7¼"h x 4¾"d

Supplies: Worsted weight yarn or Needloft® Plastic Canvas Yarn (refer to color key), two 10½" x 13½" sheets of 7 mesh plastic canvas, and #16 tapestry needle

Stitches Used: Backstitch, Overcast Stitch, Seashell Stitch, and Tent Stitch

Instructions: Photo model was stitched using worsted weight yarn. Follow charts to work Tent Stitches on Seashell Basket pieces. Refer to Stitch Diagrams (Figs. 25 and 26, page 94) to work peach Seashell Stitches. Use color to match closest stitching area to join Long Sides to Short Sides. Follow charts to work Backstitches on Handle and Sides, continuing Backstitches across joined areas of Sides. For Bottom, cut a piece of plastic canvas 62 x 32 threads. (**Note:** Bottom is not worked.) Use ecru to join Sides to Bottom. Use green and match ▲'s to join Handle to Short Sides.

Seashell Basket design by Susan Carnes.

NL	COLOR
✎	39 ecru - 30 yds
✎	53 green - 6 yds
✎	56 peach - 21 yds

Short Side (32 x 19 threads) (Work 2)

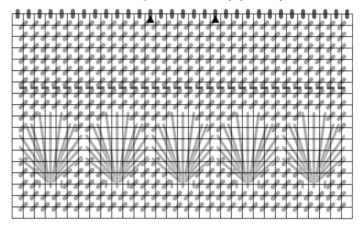

Handle (91 x 8 threads)

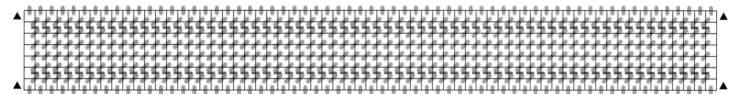

Long Side (62 x 19 threads) (Work 2)

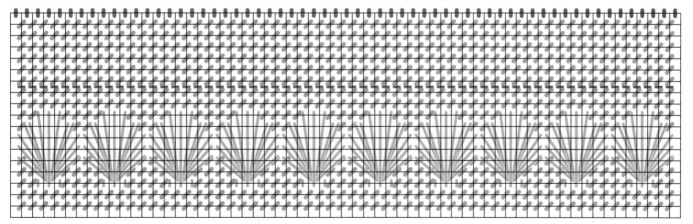

CACTUS COASTERS

Skill Level: Advanced

Size: 4"w x 4"h each

Supplies: Worsted weight yarn or Needloft® Plastic Canvas Yarn (refer to color key), one 10½" x 13½" sheet of 7 mesh plastic canvas, #16 tapestry needle, cork or felt (optional), and clear-drying craft glue

Stitches Used: Backstitch, Braided Cross Stitch Variation, Cross Stitch, Lazy Daisy Stitch, and Tent Stitch

Instructions: Photo models were stitched using worsted weight yarn. Follow charts and use required stitches to work Coaster. Use tan Braided Cross Stitch Variation to cover unworked edges of Coaster. For backing, cut cork or felt slightly smaller than Coaster and glue to wrong side of stitched piece.

Cactus Coasters designs by Mary Mohrman.

NL	COLOR
05	pink - 2 yds
39	ecru - 11 yds
43	tan - 6 yds
53	green - 6 yds
	dk green - 2 yds
05	pink Lazy Daisy

Barrel Cactus (27 x 27 threads)

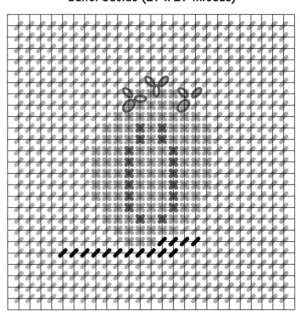

Prickly Pear Cactus (27 x 27 threads)

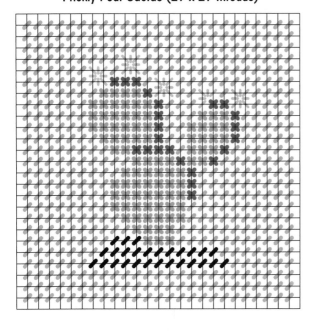

Saguaro Cactus (27 x 27 threads)

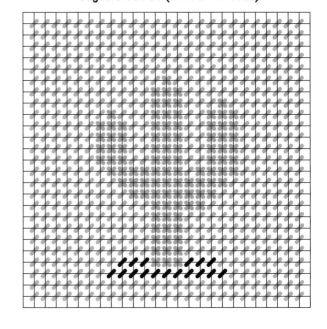

PATRIOTIC STAR BOX

Skill Level: Intermediate
Size: 5½"w x 5½"h x 2½"d
Supplies: Worsted weight yarn or Needloft® Plastic Canvas Yarn (refer to color key), one 10½" x 13½" sheet of 7 mesh plastic canvas, two Uniek® 5" plastic canvas star shapes, and #16 tapestry needle
Stitches Used: Backstitch, Overcast Stitch, Smyrna Cross Stitch, and Tent Stitch
Instructions: Photo model was stitched using worsted weight yarn. For Bottom, refer to pink cutting line on chart to cut one thread from outer edge of one star shape. (**Note:** Bottom is not worked.) For Top, trim hanger from 5" star shape. Follow charts and use required stitches to work Patriotic Star Box pieces, leaving stitches in shaded areas unworked. Use yarn color to continue stripes and match ◆'s and ✪'s to join Bottom Side A pieces to Bottom. Use yarn color to continue stripes and match ✳'s and ✛'s to join Bottom Side B pieces to Bottom. Work stitches in shaded areas to join Bottom Side pieces together. Use white to join Top Sides along short unworked edges. Work stitches in shaded area to join Top Sides to Top.

Patriotic Star Box design by Teal Lee Elliott.

NL	COLOR
02	red - 26 yds
32	blue - 5 yds
41	white - 25 yds

Bottom Side A
(11 x 16 threads)
(Work 5)

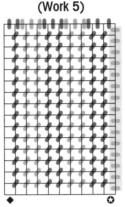

Bottom Side B
(11 x 16 threads)
(Work 5)

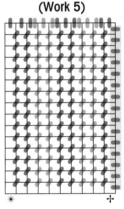

Top Side
(12 x 6 threads)
(Work 10)

Top

Bottom

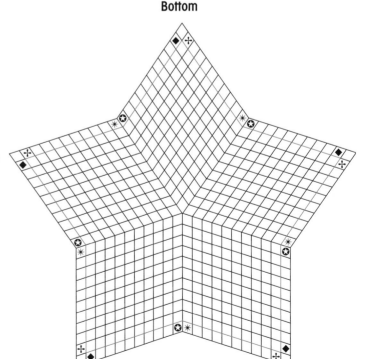

FOOD MAGNETS
Skill Level: Beginner
Jar Size: 2"w x 3¼"h each
Watermelon Size: 2¾"w x 1¾"h
Supplies: Worsted weight yarn or Needloft® Plastic Canvas Yarn (refer to color key), one 10½" x 13½" sheet of 7 mesh plastic canvas, #16 tapestry needle, ⅛"w white grosgrain ribbon, black felt, magnetic strip, and clear-drying craft glue
Stitches Used: Backstitch, Cashmere Stitch, Gobelin Stitch, Mosaic Stitch, Overcast Stitch, and Tent Stitch
Instructions: Photo models were stitched using worsted weight yarn. Follow charts and use required stitches to work desired Magnets. Glue magnetic strip to wrong side of each stitched piece. **For Jar Magnets only**, photocopy labels and trim inside border. Glue to stitched piece. Tie ribbon in a bow and trim ends. Refer to photo for placement to glue ribbon to Jars. **For Watermelon only**, use pattern to cut Watermelon Seeds from felt. Refer to photo for placement and glue Seeds to Watermelon.

Canning Jar designs by Nova Barta.
Watermelon design by Colleen Benton.

WREATH
Skill Level: Beginner
Size: 16" dia
Supplies: Worsted weight yarn or Needloft® Plastic Canvas Yarn (refer to color key), one 10½" x 13½" sheet of 7 mesh plastic canvas, #16 tapestry needle, ⅛"w white grosgrain ribbon, black felt, 16" dia grapevine wreath, assorted small baskets, 1"w craft ribbon, assorted greenery sprigs, and clear-drying craft glue
Stitches Used: Backstitch, Cashmere Stitch, Gobelin Stitch, Mosaic Stitch, Overcast Stitch, and Tent Stitch
Instructions: Photo model was stitched using worsted weight yarn. Follow charts and use required stitches to work desired designs. Refer to photo for placement and glue craft ribbon, greenery, baskets, and stitched pieces to wreath. **For Jars only**, photocopy labels and trim inside border. Glue to stitched piece. Tie ribbon in a bow and trim ends. Refer to photo for placement to glue ribbon to Jars. **For Watermelon only**, use pattern to cut Watermelon Seeds from felt. Refer to photo for placement and glue Seeds to Watermelon.

NL	COLOR
00	black
01	red
27	green
29	dk green
32	blue
41	white
52	orange
57	yellow

Jar Labels

Carrots Beans

Corn Pickles

Watermelon Seeds

Watermelon (19 x 12 threads)
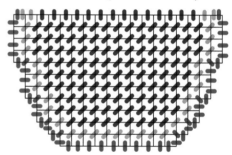

Carrots (13 x 22 threads)
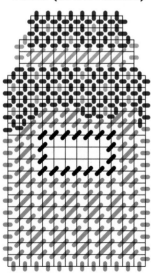

Beans (13 x 22 threads)
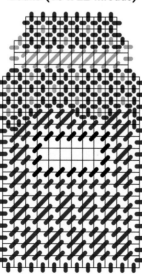

Corn (13 x 22 threads)
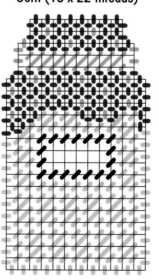

Pickles (13 x 22 threads)
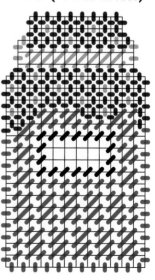

JAR LIDS

Skill Level: Beginner

Size: 3¼" dia each

Supplies: Worsted weight yarn or Needloft® Plastic Canvas Yarn (refer to color key), one 10½" x 13½" sheet of 7 mesh plastic canvas, #16 tapestry needle, 1" dia brown pom-pom, large-mouth jar lid ring (3" dia opening), and clear-drying craft glue

Stitches Used: Gobelin Stitch, Overcast Stitch, Smyrna Cross Stitch, Tent Stitch, and Turkey Loop Stitch

Instructions: Photo models were stitched using worsted weight yarn. Follow charts and use required stitches to work desired Jar Lid. Glue Jar Lid into jar lid ring. **For Sunflower only**, glue pom-pom to center of sunflower.

Sunflower Jar Lid design by Joan Bartling.
Cow Spots Jar Lid design by Rose Munz.
Patriotic Jar Lid design by Josette Land.

NL	COLOR
✏	00 black
✏	01 red
✏	32 blue
✏	41 white
○	57 yellow Turkey Loop

Patriotic Jar Lid (22 x 22 threads)

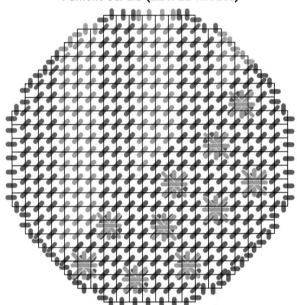

Cow Spots Jar Lid (22 x 22 threads)

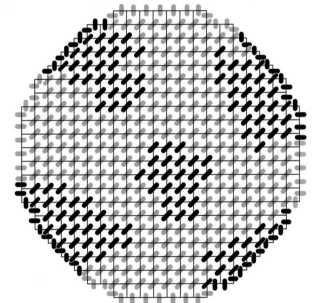

Sunflower Jar Lid (22 x 22 threads)

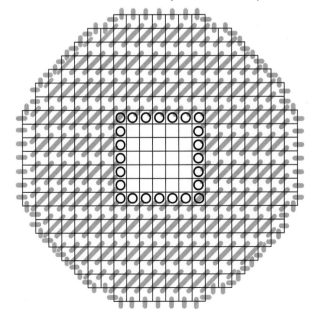

AUTUMN

A cornucopia of rich color announces the arrival of autumn, bringing with it familiar customs such as giving thanks, gathering pumpkins, and trick-or-treating. A crop of golden pumpkins graces our wall hanging and tissue box cover. The coordinating quilt-block magnet is a kaleidoscope of spectacular autumn hues. This collection celebrates all the things we like best about autumn — the glory of the harvest, brilliant leaves, and special holidays.

Autumn signals back-to-school time, and our pencil-shaped magnet (right) makes a point of posting important school papers in a prominent place. Our handy lunch tote and apple-shaped bag clip (below) are a great surprise for a child's favorite teacher. She can even use the tote to carry school papers home for grading. Our bewitching pencil toppers (opposite, top) are sure to cast a playful spell on the school day. The frightening foursome is perfect for spooky party favors, too! Our musical haunted house (opposite, bottom) offers a fun way to display your plastic canvas trickery, and you can choose your favorite spooky tune.

74

String a crop of colorful plastic canvas pumpkins together to create our autumn garland (opposite, top). Chenille stem cattails add a realistic touch to our Canada goose doorstop (opposite, bottom), which brings the beauty of the Great Outdoors into your home. Standing guard over a pumpkin patch strewn with excelsior and leaves, our friendly scarecrow (below) makes an adorable autumn centerpiece.

Reflecting the glory of autumn leaves, our coaster set (opposite, top) is given two spectacular looks by simply changing the background color. The coordinating magnets (below) are handy for posting notes and "to-do" lists. The striking formation of migrating geese was the inspiration for the pattern on our tissue box cover (opposite, bottom). Fashioned in honor of the men and women who founded our great country, the Pilgrim figures (left) will lend traditional appeal to your Thanksgiving celebration.

NL COLOR
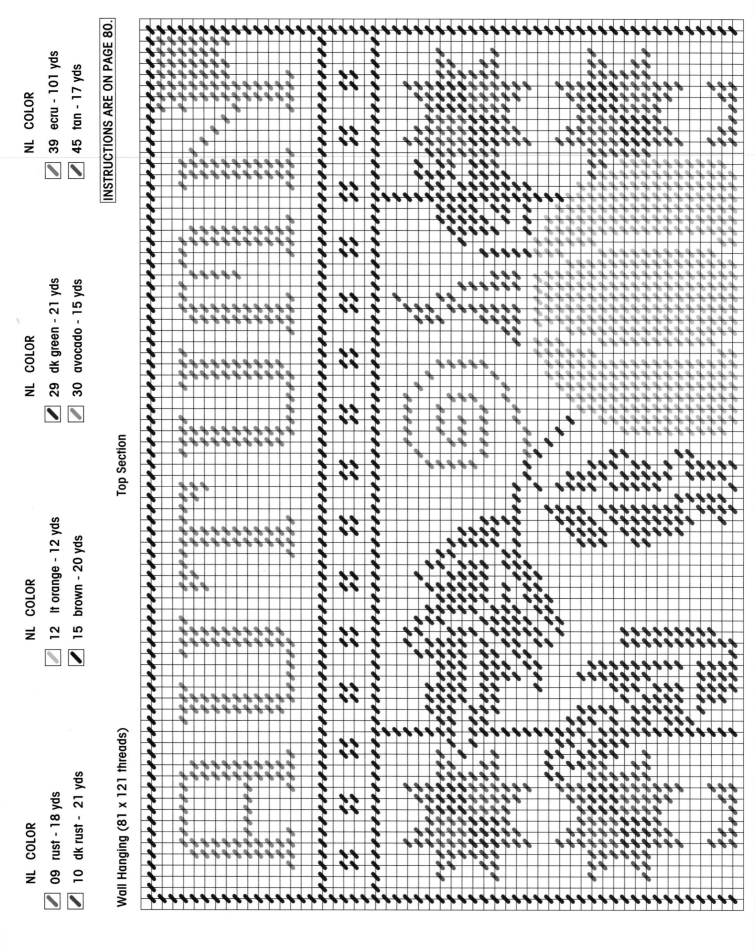

NL	COLOR	
◢	09	rust - 18 yds
◢	10	dk rust - 21 yds

NL	COLOR	
◢	12	lt orange - 12 yds
◢	15	brown - 20 yds

NL	COLOR	
◢	29	dk green - 21 yds
◢	30	avocado - 15 yds

NL	COLOR	
◢	39	ecru - 101 yds
◢	45	tan - 17 yds

INSTRUCTIONS ARE ON PAGE 80.

Top Section

Wall Hanging (81 x 121 threads)

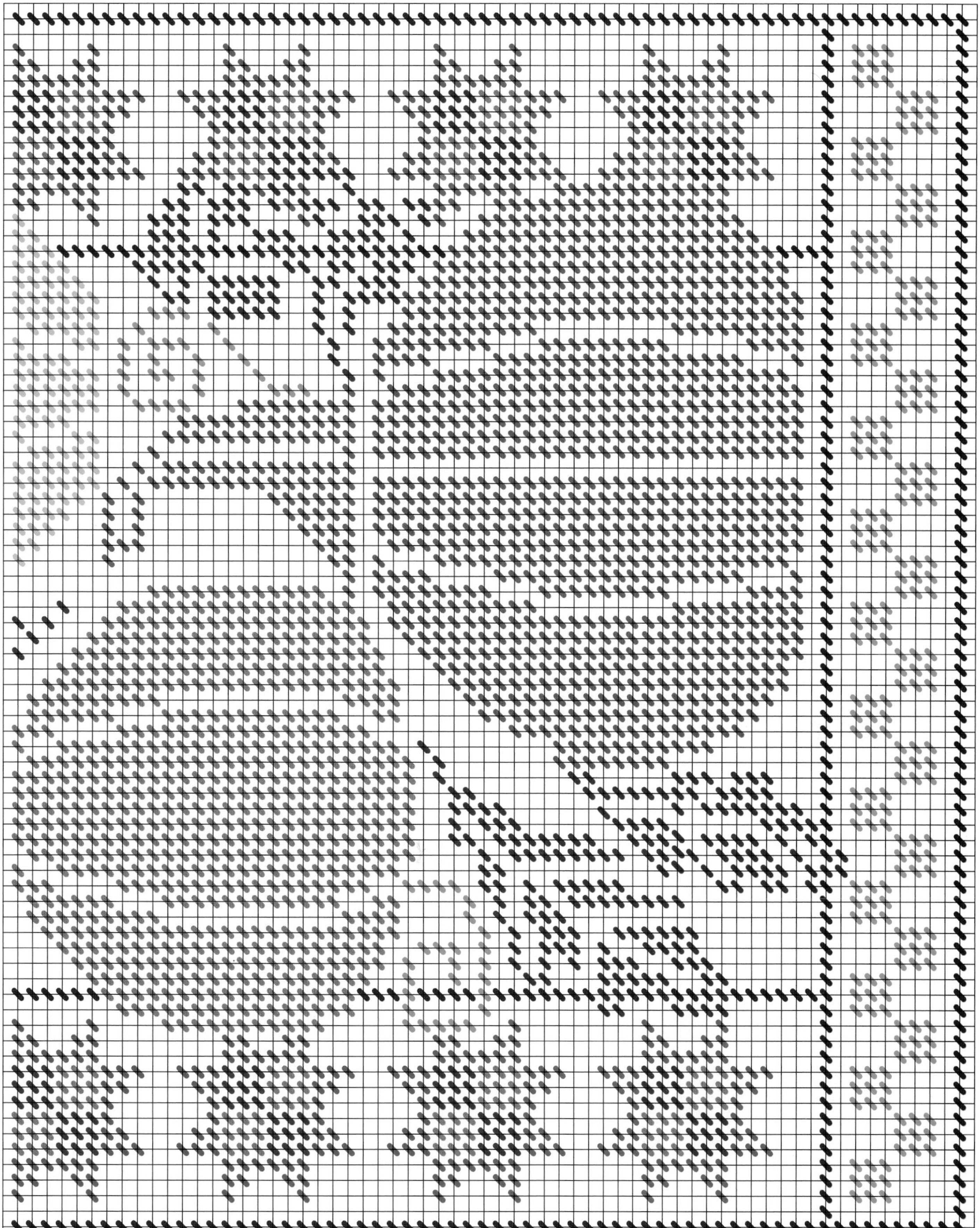

Bottom Section

AUTUMN WALL HANGING

Skill Level: Intermediate
Size: 12"w x 18"h
Supplies: Needloft® Plastic Canvas Yarn or worsted weight yarn (refer to color key), one 12" x 18" sheet of 7 mesh plastic canvas, #16 tapestry needle, sewing needle and thread, and sawtooth hanger
Stitches Used: Overcast Stitch and Tent Stitch
Instructions: Photo model was stitched using Needloft® Plastic Canvas Yarn. (**Note:** Design fits a 12" x 18" sheet of canvas.) Follow chart and use required stitches to work Top Section. Follow chart and use required stitches to work Bottom Section below Top Section. Complete background with ecru Tent Stitches as indicated on chart. Use ecru Overcast Stitches to cover unworked edges. Use sewing needle and thread to attach sawtooth hanger to wrong side of stitched piece.

AUTUMN TISSUE BOX COVER

Skill Level: Beginner
Size: 4½"w x 5¾"h x 4½"d
(**Note:** Fits a 4¼"w x 5¼"h x 4¼"d boutique tissue box.)
Supplies: Needloft® Plastic Canvas Yarn or worsted weight yarn (refer to color key), one 10½" x 13½" sheet of 7 mesh plastic canvas, and #16 tapestry needle
Stitches Used: Overcast Stitch and Tent Stitch
Instructions: Photo model was stitched using Needloft® Plastic Canvas Yarn. Follow charts and use required stitches to work Tissue Box Cover pieces. Complete backgrounds with ecru Tent Stitches as indicated on charts. Use brown for all joining. Join Sides along long edges. Join Top to Sides.

AUTUMN MAGNET

Skill Level: Beginner
Size: 2"w x 2"h
Supplies: Needloft® Plastic Canvas Yarn or worsted weight yarn (refer to color key), one 10½" x 13½" sheet of 7 mesh plastic canvas, #16 tapestry needle, magnetic strip, and clear-drying craft glue
Stitches Used: Overcast Stitch and Tent Stitch
Instructions: Photo model was stitched using Needloft® Plastic Canvas Yarn. Follow chart and use required stitches to work Magnet. Glue magnetic strip to wrong side of stitched piece.

Autumn Set designs by Polly Carbonari.

NL	COLOR
09	rust - 21 yds
12	lt orange - 15 yds
15	brown - 21 yds
29	dk green - 16 yds
39	ecru - 45 yds
43	tan - 5 yds

Magnet (14 x 14 threads)

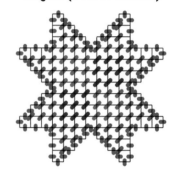

Tissue Box Cover Side (30 x 38 threads) (Work 4)

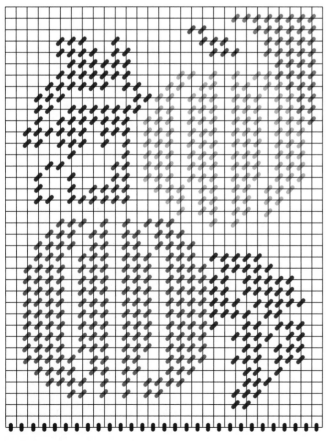

Tissue Box Cover Top (30 x 30 threads)

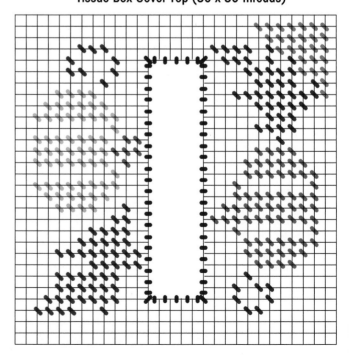

LEAF COASTER
Skill Level: Beginner
Size: 4¹⁄₂"w x 4¹⁄₂"h each

Supplies: Needloft® Plastic Canvas Yarn or worsted weight yarn (refer to color key), one 10¹⁄₂" x 13¹⁄₂" sheet of 7 mesh plastic canvas, #16 tapestry needle, cork or felt, and clear-drying craft glue
Stitches Used: Backstitch, Gobelin Stitch, Overcast Stitch, and Tent Stitch
Instructions: Photo models were stitched using Needloft® Plastic Canvas Yarn. Work stitches indicated by double lines on chart by inserting needle in same holes twice for complete coverage. Follow chart and use required stitches to work Leaf Coaster. For backing, cut cork or felt slightly smaller than stitched piece. Glue cork or felt to wrong side of Coaster.

LEAF MAGNET
Skill Level: Beginner
Size: 2³⁄₄"w x 2³⁄₄"h each

Supplies: Needloft® Plastic Canvas Yarn or worsted weight yarn (refer to color key), one 10¹⁄₂" x 13¹⁄₂" sheet of 7 mesh plastic canvas, #16 tapestry needle, magnetic strip, and clear-drying craft glue
Stitches Used: Backstitch, Gobelin Stitch, Overcast Stitch, and Tent Stitch
Instructions: Photo models were stitched using Needloft® Plastic Canvas Yarn. Work stitches indicated by double lines on chart by inserting needle in same holes twice for complete coverage. Follow chart and use required stitches to work Leaf Magnet. Glue magnetic strip to wrong side of stitched piece.

Leaf Coaster and Leaf Magnet designs by Betty Reinkoester.

NL	COLOR
10	rust
12	orange
17	gold
30	dk green
	background color
	leaf color

Leaf Magnet (16 x 16 threads)

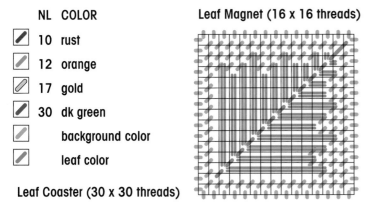

Leaf Coaster (30 x 30 threads)

HALLOWEEN PENCIL TOPPERS
Skill Level: Beginner
Approx Size: 2¹⁄₂"w x 2¹⁄₂"h each

Supplies: Worsted weight yarn or Needloft® Plastic Canvas Yarn (refer to color key), one 10¹⁄₂" x 13¹⁄₂" sheet of 7 mesh plastic canvas, #16 tapestry needle, two 7mm black glass beads, and two 7mm moving eyes
Stitches Used: French Knot, Fringe, Overcast Stitch, and Tent Stitch
Instructions: Photo models were stitched using worsted weight yarn. Follow chart and use required stitches to work desired Pencil Topper. Use yarn color to match closest stitching area and match ▲'s to join ends. **For Witch only,** trim Fringe to 1¹⁄₂". Separate yarn ends into plies.

Halloween Pencil Topper designs by Linda Smith.

NL	COLOR		NL	COLOR
00	black		27	green Fr. Knot
27	green		52	orange Fringe
41	white			bead placement
52	orange			

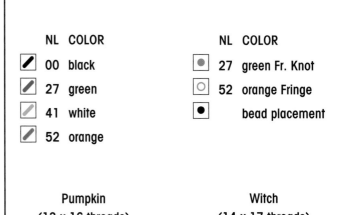

Pumpkin
(13 x 16 threads)

Witch
(14 x 17 threads)

Ghost
(11 x 17 threads)

Bat
(18 x 14 threads)

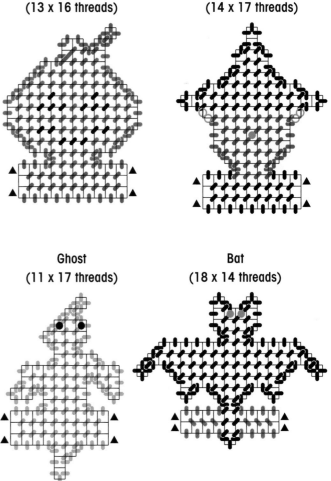

PILGRIM FIGURES
Skill Level: Intermediate
Supplies For Entire Set: Worsted weight yarn or Needloft® Plastic Canvas Yarn (refer to color key), DMC embroidery floss (refer to color key), two 10½" x 13½" sheets of 7 mesh plastic canvas, one 10½" x 13½" sheet of 10 mesh plastic canvas, #16 tapestry needle, #20 tapestry needle, and clear-drying craft glue
Stitches Used For Entire Set: Backstitch, French Knot, Gobelin Stitch, Mosaic Stitch, Overcast Stitch, Scotch Stitch, and Tent Stitch

PILGRIM WOMAN
Size: 9⅜"h x 2" dia
Instructions: Photo model was stitched using worsted weight yarn and embroidery floss. Use yarn for 7 mesh plastic canvas and 12 strands of embroidery floss for 10 mesh plastic canvas. Follow charts and use required stitches to work Basket on 10 mesh plastic canvas and remaining pieces on 7 mesh plastic canvas. Refer to photo for placement to assemble pieces. Use color to match closest stitching area for all joining and tacking. Join Pilgrim Woman along unworked edges, forming a cylinder. Cut a 10" length of ecru yarn. Thread yarn through Apron at +'s. Match +'s to place Apron on Pilgrim Woman. To secure Apron to Pilgrim Woman, wrap yarn around Pilgrim Woman and tie in a bow at back of Pilgrim Woman. Match ▲'s to tack Arms to Pilgrim Woman. Glue Basket to Arms. Slide Collar over Pilgrim Woman. Tack Collar to Pilgrim Woman and Arms. Match ★'s to join Bonnet Back to Bonnet along unworked edges. Tack Bonnet to Pilgrim Woman.

PILGRIM MAN
Size: 10½"h x 1½" dia
Instructions: Photo model was stitched using worsted weight yarn and embroidery floss. Use yarn for 7 mesh plastic canvas and 12 strands of embroidery floss for 10 mesh plastic canvas. Follow charts and use required stitches to work Buckles, Pumpkin, and Leaf on 10 mesh plastic canvas and remaining pieces on 7 mesh plastic canvas. Refer to photo for placement to assemble pieces. Use color to match closest stitching area for all joining and tacking. Join Pilgrim Man along unworked edges, forming a cylinder. Glue one Buckle to Pilgrim Man in center front of black belt. Glue Cuffs to Arms. Match ▲'s to tack Arms to Pilgrim Man. Join Collar along unworked edges. Slide Collar over Pilgrim Man. Slide Hat Brim over Pilgrim Man and tack in place. Glue remaining Buckle to hat. Glue Leaf to Pumpkin. Glue Pumpkin to Arms.

Pilgrim Figure designs by Becky Dill.

NL	COLOR
00	black - 2 yds
07	pink - 1 yd
13	brown - 4 yds
37	grey - 10 yds
38	dk grey - 12 yds
39	ecru - 7 yds
56	flesh - 3 yds
	gold* - 3 yds
●	gold Fr. Knot*
●	blue Fr. Knot* - 1 yd

*Use 2-ply yarn.

DMC	COLOR
300	dk brown - 3 yds
319	green - 2 yds
321	red - 3 yds
946	orange - 3 yds

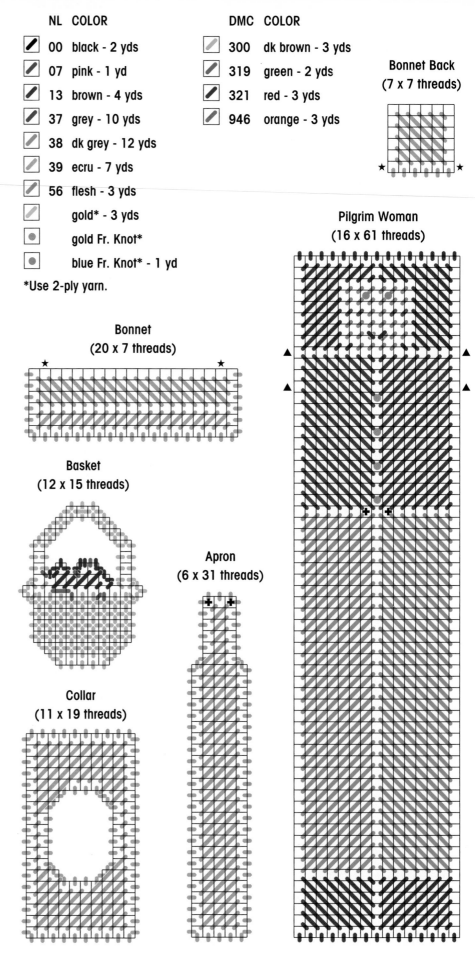

Bonnet Back
(7 x 7 threads)

Pilgrim Woman
(16 x 61 threads)

Bonnet
(20 x 7 threads)

Basket
(12 x 15 threads)

Apron
(6 x 31 threads)

Collar
(11 x 19 threads)

Arms (38 x 4 threads) (Work 2)

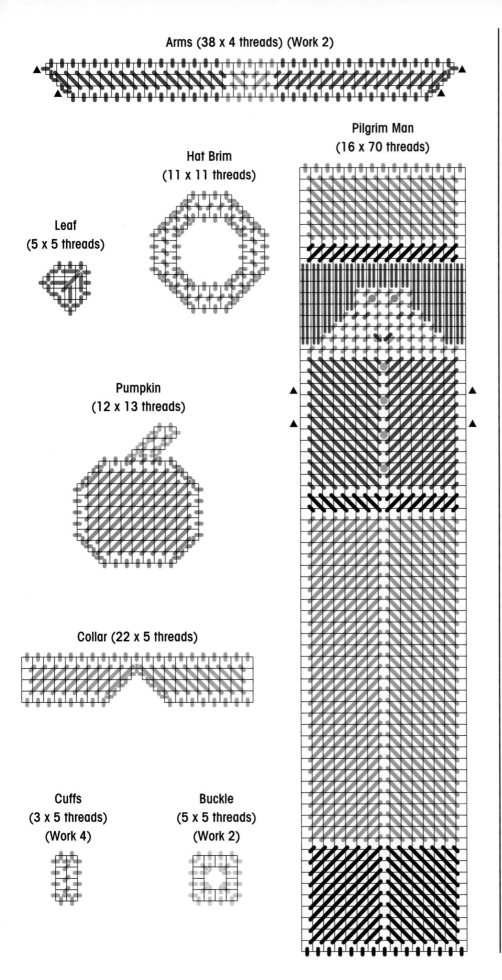

**Hat Brim
(11 x 11 threads)**

**Leaf
(5 x 5 threads)**

**Pilgrim Man
(16 x 70 threads)**

**Pumpkin
(12 x 13 threads)**

Collar (22 x 5 threads)

**Cuffs
(3 x 5 threads)
(Work 4)**

**Buckle
(5 x 5 threads)
(Work 2)**

PENCIL MAGNET
Skill Level: Beginner
Size: 1⅝"w x 4½"h
Supplies: Needloft® Plastic Canvas Yarn or worsted weight yarn (refer to color key), one 10½" x 13½" sheet of 7 mesh plastic canvas, #16 tapestry needle, magnetic strip, and clear-drying craft glue
Stitches Used: Gobelin Stitch, Overcast Stitch, and Tent Stitch
Instructions: Photo model was stitched using worsted weight yarn. Follow chart and use required stitches to work Pencil Magnet. Glue magnetic strip to wrong side of stitched piece.

Pencil Magnet design by Diane Villano.

NL	COLOR
00	black - 1 yd
12	gold - 3 yds
16	tan - 1 yd
37	grey - 1 yd
55	pink - 1 yd

**Pencil Magnet
(13 x 29 threads)**

PUMPKIN GARLAND

Skill Level: Advanced
Pumpkin #1 Size: 3³/₈"w x 4³/₄"h x ¹/₂"d
Pumpkin #2 Size: 4¹/₄"w x 5⁵/₈"h x ¹/₂"d
Pumpkin #3 Size: 2⁷/₈"w x 3¹/₄"h x ¹/₂"d
Supplies: Worsted weight yarn or Needloft® Plastic Canvas yarn (refer to color keys), two 10¹/₂" x 13¹/₂" sheets of 7 mesh plastic canvas, #16 tapestry needle, polyester fiberfill, artificial leaves, natural jute, and clear-drying craft glue
Stitches Used: Gobelin Stitch, Overcast Stitch, and Tent Stitch
Instructions: Photo model was stitched using worsted weight yarn. Follow charts and use required stitches to work one Pumpkin #2 and two each of Pumpkin #1 and Pumpkin #3. For Back of Pumpkins, cut one Pumpkin #2 and two each of Pumpkin #1 and Pumpkin #3. Turn Backs over. (Stems on Pumpkin #1 and Pumpkin #2 Backs will curve to the left.) Follow Pumpkin charts to work Backs in mirror image of Fronts. With wrong sides together, use yarn color to match closest stitching area to join Fronts to Backs while lightly stuffing with polyester fiberfill. Cut a length of jute the desired Garland length plus 8". Fold jute in half to find the center. Glue center of jute to wrong side of Pumpkin #2. Refer to photo for placement to glue remaining Pumpkins to jute. Glue leaves to Garland. Making a 1" loop, tie each end of jute in a knot and trim ends.

SCARECROW CENTERPIECE

Skill Level: Advanced
Approx Size: 17"h x 14" dia
Supplies: Worsted weight yarn or Needloft® Plastic Canvas yarn (refer to color keys), Darice® Tan Straw Satin Raffia, four 10¹/₂" x 13¹/₂" sheets of 7 mesh plastic canvas, #16 tapestry needle, 12" of ¹/₂"w orange satin ribbon, polyester fiberfill, 12" dia straw wreath, 1"h x 6" dia Styrofoam™ circle, five 6" floral picks, excelsior, natural raffia, artificial leaves, 8" dia straw hat, 10mm oval moving eyes, and clear-drying craft glue
Stitches Used: Backstitch, Cross Stitch, Gobelin Stitch, Mosaic Stitch, Overcast Stitch, Tent Stitch, and Turkey Loop Stitch
Instructions: Photo model was stitched using worsted weight yarn. Follow charts and use required stitches to work Scarecrow and Crow pieces. Work stitches indicated by double lines on chart by inserting needle in same holes twice for complete coverage. Work one each of Pumpkin #1, Pumpkin #2, and Pumpkin #3. For Back of Pumpkins, cut one each of Pumpkin #1, Pumpkin #2, and Pumpkin #3. Turn Backs over. (Stems on Pumpkin #1 and Pumpkin #2 Backs will curve to the left.) Follow Pumpkin charts to work Backs in mirror image of Fronts.

Refer to photo for placement and use tan to tack Buttons to Scarecrow Front. Use white to tack Patch to Scarecrow Front. With wrong sides together, use yarn color to match closest stitching area to join Scarecrow Front to Scarecrow Back while lightly stuffing with polyester fiberfill. Leave bottom edges of Scarecrow open between ✦'s. Use brown and match ✦'s to join

Shoe Soles to Scarecrow Front and Back. Insert a floral pick inside heels of Scarecrow feet, leaving 2" of each floral pick extending below Scarecrow. Tie ribbon in a bow and trim ends. Glue bow to Scarecrow Front. Glue hat to Scarecrow.
For Crow, refer to photo for placement and use gold to tack Beak to Crow Front. Use tan to tack Feet to Crow Front. With wrong sides together, use black to join Crow Front to Crow Back. Glue moving eyes to Crow Front. Use black to tack Crow to Scarecrow.
For each Pumpkin, glue one floral pick to wrong side of Back, leaving 2" of floral pick extending below Pumpkin. With wrong sides together, use yarn color to match closest stitching area to join Front to Back while lightly stuffing with polyester fiberfill.
Refer to photo for placement to assemble Centerpiece. For base, cut Styrofoam to fit inside wreath. Glue Styrofoam to inside of wreath. Glue excelsior to Styrofoam and wreath. To attach stitched pieces to base, apply glue to floral picks extending from stitched pieces and insert floral picks into base. Pumpkins may be displayed facing any direction. (**Note:** Additional glue may be used along bottom edges of stitched pieces to attach to base.) Glue leaves to base. Tie raffia in a bow and glue bow to base.

Pumpkin Garland and Scarecrow Centerpiece designs by Peggy Astle.

NL	COLOR
✎	00 black
✎	15 brown
✎	16 tan
✎	17 gold
✎	29 green
✎	33 blue
✎	41 white
✎	47 flesh
✎	48 dk blue
✎	terra-cotta
✎	dk terra-cotta
○	Straw Satin Raffia Turkey Loop

Pumpkin #1 (23 x 32 threads)

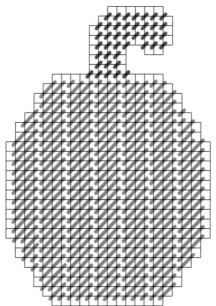

Pumpkin #2 (28 x 38 threads)

Shoe Sole (21 x 7 threads) (Work 2)

Beak (5 x 5 threads)

Patch (11 x 12 threads)

Scarecrow Front (69 x 88 threads)

Crow Front/Back (17 x 23 threads)
(Work 2)

Button (6 x 6 threads)
(Work 2)

Feet (11 x 7 threads)

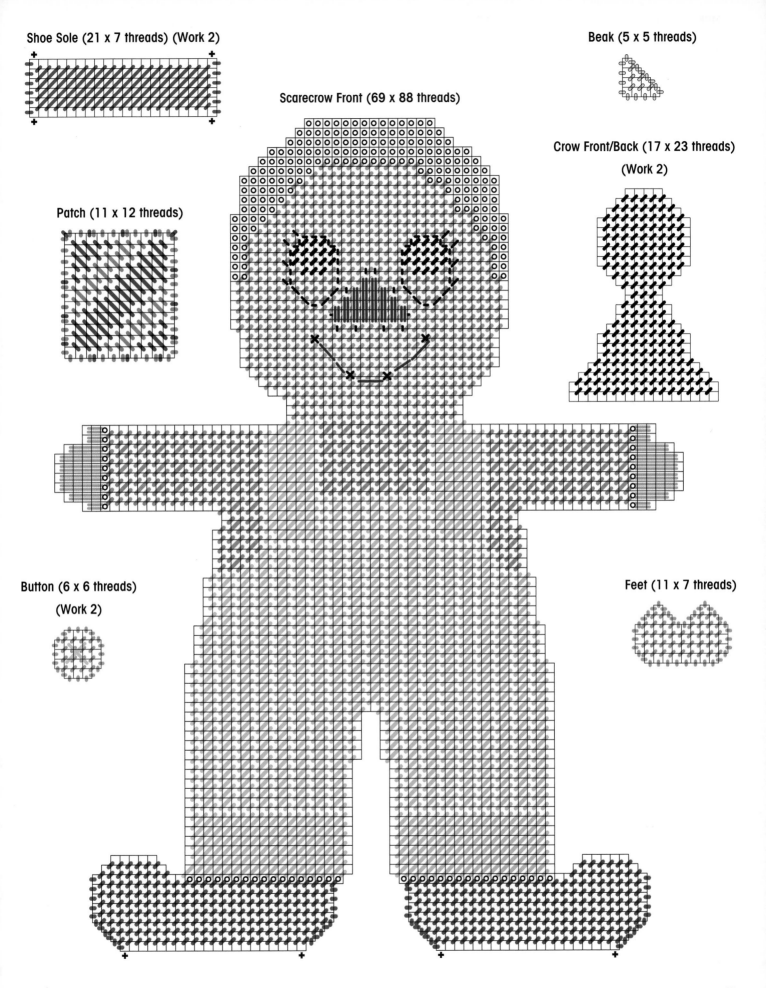

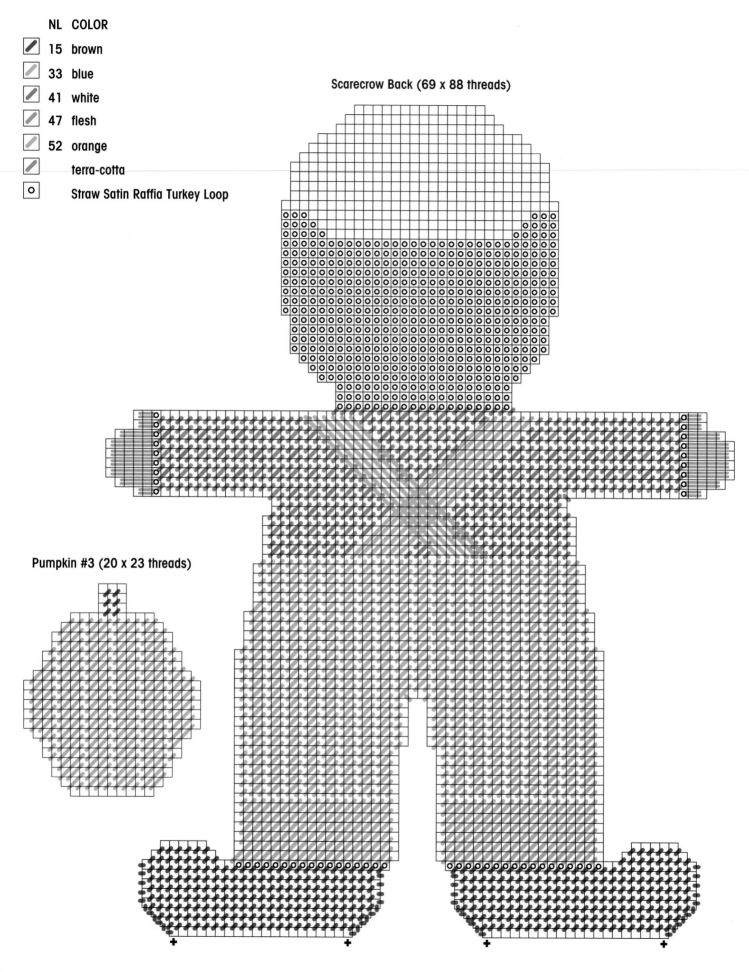

NL COLOR

15 brown

33 blue

41 white

47 flesh

52 orange

terra-cotta

○ Straw Satin Raffia Turkey Loop

Scarecrow Back (69 x 88 threads)

Pumpkin #3 (20 x 23 threads)

CANADA GOOSE DOORSTOP

Skill Level: Intermediate

Size: 14"w x 8½"h x 3½"d

(**Note:** Holds a 8"w x 3⅝"h x 2⅛"d brick.)

Supplies: Worsted weight yarn or Needloft® Plastic Canvas Yarn (refer to color key), three 10½" x 13½" sheets of 7 mesh plastic canvas, three 10" wooden skewers, five 6mm brown chenille stems, #16 tapestry needle, brick, nylon line, plastic wrap, and clear-drying craft glue

Stitches Used: Backstitch, Gobelin Stitch, Overcast Stitch, and Tent Stitch

Instructions: Photo model was stitched using worsted weight yarn. For Doorstop Front and Back, cut two pieces of plastic canvas 57 x 27 threads each. For Long Sides, cut two pieces of plastic canvas 57 x 17 threads each. For Short Sides, cut two pieces of plastic canvas 17 x 27 threads each. Work green slanting Gobelin Stitches over two threads to cover Front, Back, and Sides. Follow charts and use required stitches to work remaining Canada Goose Doorstop pieces. Use lt green and match like symbols to tack Leaves to Goose. Use green for remainder of joining. Join Long Sides to Short Sides along short edges. Join Front to Sides. Use nylon line to tack Goose to Front. Wrap brick with plastic wrap. Place brick inside Doorstop. Join Back to Sides. For cattails, cut skewers into three 4" sections, one 4½" section, and one 5½" section. Wrap one chenille stem around the end of each skewer section and secure using glue. Refer to photo for placement and glue skewers to Goose.

	NL	COLOR
![black]	00	black - 4 yds
![tan]	16	tan - 4 yds
![gold]	17	gold - 1 yd
![lt green]	26	lt green - 6 yds
![green]	29	green - 49 yds

	NL	COLOR
![grey blue]	34	grey blue - 2 yds
![grey]	38	grey - 1 yd
![white]	41	white - 3 yds
![brown]	43	brown - 1 yd

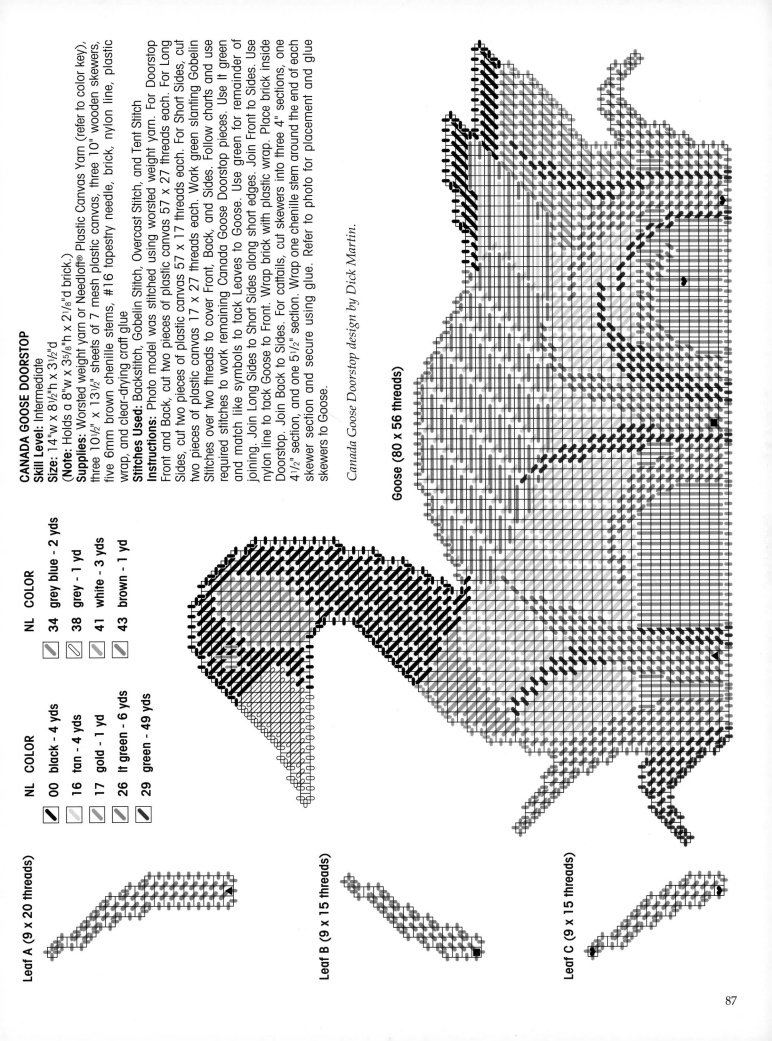

Goose (80 x 56 threads)

Canada Goose Doorstop design by Dick Martin.

Leaf A (9 x 20 threads)

Leaf B (9 x 15 threads)

Leaf C (9 x 15 threads)

APPLE CHIP CLIP
Skill Level: Beginner
Size: 3"w x 3⅛"h
Supplies: Needloft® Plastic Canvas Yarn or worsted weight yarn (refer to color key), one 10½" x 13½" sheet of 7 mesh plastic canvas, #16 tapestry needle, 3¼" long wooden clothespin (may be stained), and clear-drying craft glue
Stitches Used: Backstitch, Gobelin Stitch, Overcast Stitch, and Tent Stitch
Instructions: Photo model was stitched using Needloft® Plastic Canvas Yarn. Follow chart and use required stitches to work Apple Chip Clip. Glue clothespin to wrong side of stitched piece.

NL	COLOR
02	red - 4 yds
14	brown - 2 yds
27	green - 2 yds
28	lt green - 2 yds
41	white - 2 yds

Apple Chip Clip (20 x 21 threads)

"SCHOOL DAYS" TOTE
Skill Level: Intermediate
Size: 8¼"w x 15¾"h x 4"d
Supplies: Needloft® Plastic Canvas Yarn or worsted weight yarn (refer to color key), two 13⅝" x 21⅝" sheets of 5 mesh plastic canvas, and #16 tapestry needle
Stitches Used: Backstitch, Gobelin Stitch, Overcast Stitch, and Tent Stitch
Instructions: Photo model was stitched using Needloft® Plastic Canvas Yarn. Unless otherwise indicated, use two strands of yarn. Follow chart and use required stitches to work Front and Back. Before adding Backstitches, complete background with black Tent Stitches as indicated on chart. For Sides, cut two pieces of plastic canvas 20 x 46 threads each. For Bottom, cut one piece of plastic canvas 41 x 20 threads. For Handles, cut two pieces of plastic canvas 5 x 86 threads each. Work Sides, Bottom, and Handles with tan slanting Gobelin Stitches over three threads. Use tan to join Front and Back to Sides along long edges. Use tan to join Bottom to Front, Back, and Sides. Use tan Overcast Stitches to cover unworked edges of Handles. Refer to photo for placement and use tan to tack Handles to wrong side of Front and Back.

"School Days" Tote design by Michele Wilcox.

NL	COLOR
00	black - 74 yds
02	red - 25 yds
27	green - 5 yds
41	white - 13 yds
	white*
43	tan - 221 yds

*Use 1 strand of yarn.

Front/Back (41 x 46 threads)

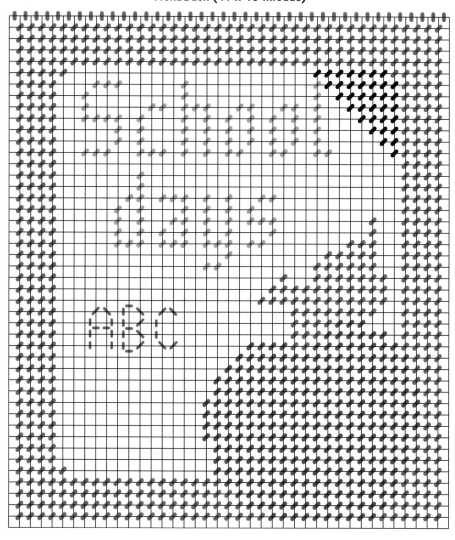

FLYING GEESE TISSUE BOX COVER

Skill Level: Beginner

Size: 4⅝"w x 5½"h x 4⅝"d

(**Note:** Fits a 4¼"w x 5¼"h x 4¼"d boutique tissue box.)

Supplies: ⅛"w double-face satin ribbon or Needloft® Plastic Canvas Yarn (refer to color key), two 10½" x 13½" sheets of 7 mesh plastic canvas, and #16 tapestry needle

Stitches Used: Gobelin Stitch, Overcast Stitch, and Tent Stitch

Instructions: Photo model was stitched using satin ribbon. Follow charts and use required stitches to work Flying Geese Tissue Box Cover pieces. Use green for all joining. Refer to photo for placement and join Sides along edges. Join Top to Sides.

Flying Geese Tissue Box Cover design by Joan Green.

NL	COLOR
10	rust - 20 yds
18	tan - 16 yds
27	green - 20 yds

Top (31 x 31 threads)

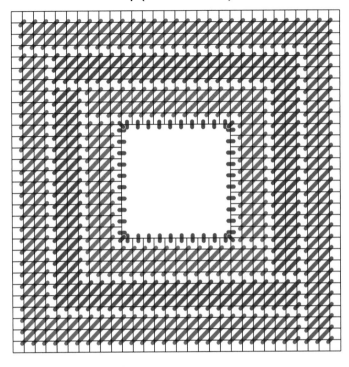

Side A (31 x 37 threads) (Work 2)

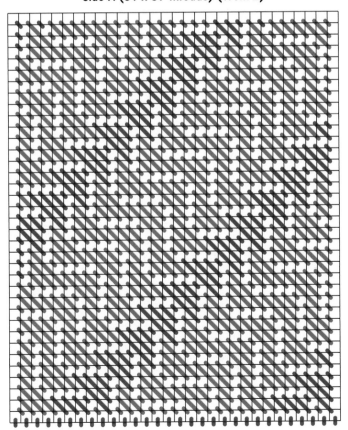

Side B (31 x 37 threads) (Work 2)

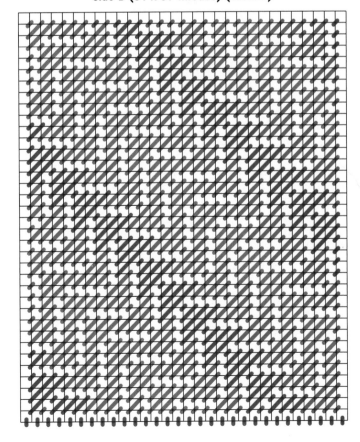

HALLOWEEN MUSIC BOX

Skill Level: Advanced
Size: 6"h x 6" dia
Supplies: Worsted weight yarn or Needloft® Plastic Canvas Yarn (refer to color key), DMC embroidery floss (refer to color key), one 12" x 18" sheet of 7 mesh plastic canvas, two 10½" x 13½" sheets of 10 mesh plastic canvas, three 9" dia plastic canvas circles, one 2⅜"w x 2"h x 1¼"d music box with rotating stand, two 2mm round gold beads, #16 tapestry needle, #20 tapestry needle, and clear-drying craft glue or hot glue gun and glue sticks
Stitches Used: Backstitch, French Knot, Gobelin Stitch, Mosaic Stitch, Overcast Stitch, and Tent Stitch

Instructions:

Photo model was stitched using worsted weight yarn and DMC embroidery floss. For Base Top, trim 12 threads from outer edge of one 9" dia plastic canvas circle. Use green yarn to work straight Gobelin Stitches over three threads to cover Base Top. For Base Side, cut a piece of 7 mesh plastic canvas 126 x 10 threads. Leave stitches in shaded areas unworked and follow chart to work Base Side. Work stitches in repeat section to cover piece. Match ▲'s and work stitches in shaded areas through two thicknesses to join ends of Base Side, forming a cylinder. Use green to join Base Side to Base Top.

For Base Bottom, trim 12 threads from outer edges of two 9" dia plastic canvas circles. (**Note:** Circles are not worked.) Cut out center intersection from circles. Push post of music box stand through the center of both circles. Remove key from music box to insert post of stand into music box. Glue top of music box to center of wrong side of Base Top. Use green yarn to join circles to bottom edge of Base Side through three thicknesses.

Cut all remaining Halloween Music Box pieces from 10 mesh plastic canvas. Use 12 strands of embroidery floss to work 10 mesh plastic canvas pieces. Use six strands of embroidery floss for Backstitch and French Knots. Follow charts and use required stitches to work remaining Halloween Music Box pieces.

Refer to Diagram on page 41 and photos for assembly. Use embroidery floss for remainder of joining. Use grey to join House Front to House Sides. Use grey and match ★'s to join Back Wall to House Sides. Use grey to join House Back to House Sides. Use black to join Roof Front to Roof Back along unworked edges. Use black to join Extension Roof pieces along unworked edges. Use orange to join long unworked edges of Chimney Sides to Chimney Front. Use orange to join remaining unworked edges of Chimney Sides to Chimney Back. Place wrong sides of Tree Front and Back together. Use brown to join Tree pieces.

Refer to photo for placement to glue Shutters to House Front, Back, and Sides. Glue Roof to House Sides. Glue Extension Roof to Back Wall and House Back. Glue Chimney to Roof. Glue one bead to each door. Glue one Ghost A and one Ghost B to Tree. Glue remaining Ghosts to Chimney and Extension Roof. Glue House, Tree, Pumpkin, Tombstone, and Fence pieces to Base Top.

Halloween Music Box design by Karen McDanel.

NL	COLOR
▨	27 green - 30 yds

DMC	COLOR
▨	blanc white - 9 yds
▨	307 yellow - 4 yds
▰	310 black - 37 yds
▨	414 grey - 43 yds
▰	700 green - 1 yd
▨	869 brown - 13 yds
▨	947 orange - 20 yds
●	310 black Fr. Knot

House Side A (22 x 28 threads)

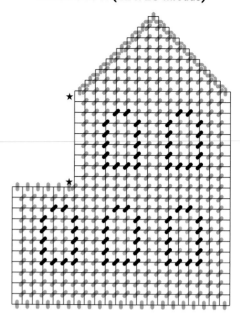

House Side B (22 x 28 threads)

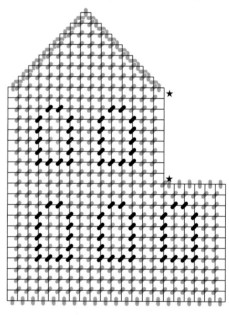

House Back (24 x 23 threads)

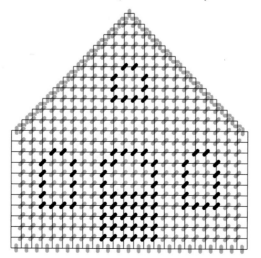

House Front (24 x 21 threads)

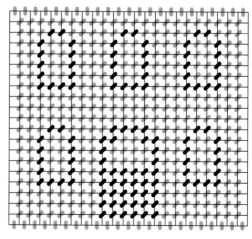

90

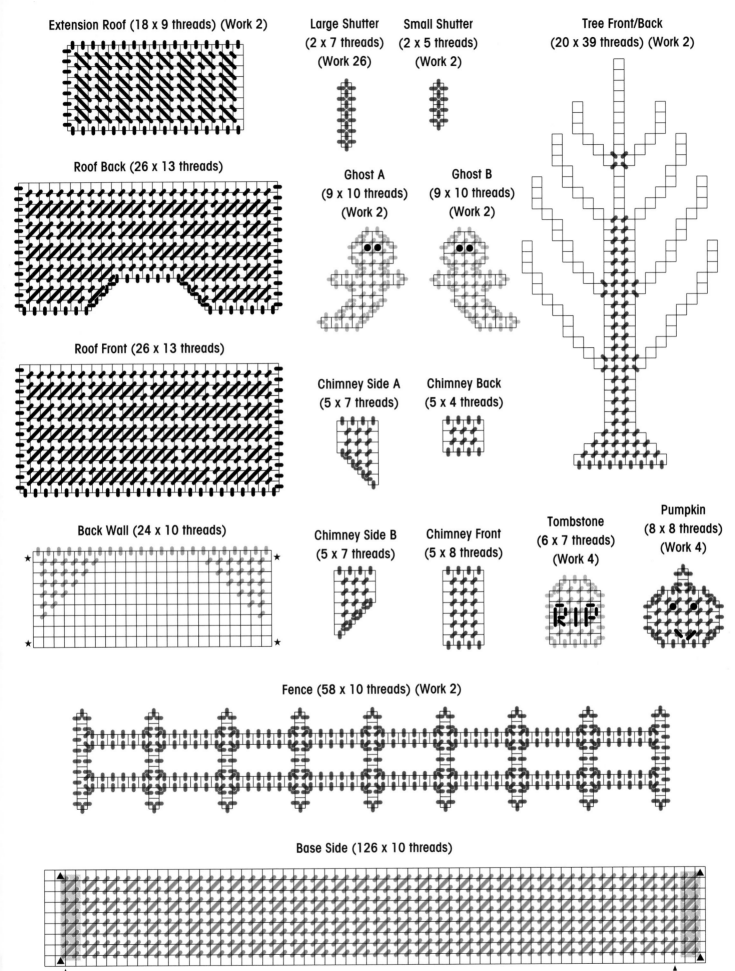

Extension Roof (18 x 9 threads) (Work 2)

Large Shutter
(2 x 7 threads)
(Work 26)

Small Shutter
(2 x 5 threads)
(Work 2)

Tree Front/Back
(20 x 39 threads) (Work 2)

Roof Back (26 x 13 threads)

Ghost A
(9 x 10 threads)
(Work 2)

Ghost B
(9 x 10 threads)
(Work 2)

Roof Front (26 x 13 threads)

Chimney Side A
(5 x 7 threads)

Chimney Back
(5 x 4 threads)

Back Wall (24 x 10 threads)

Chimney Side B
(5 x 7 threads)

Chimney Front
(5 x 8 threads)

Tombstone
(6 x 7 threads)
(Work 4)

Pumpkin
(8 x 8 threads)
(Work 4)

Fence (58 x 10 threads) (Work 2)

Base Side (126 x 10 threads)

Repeat

91

GENERAL INSTRUCTIONS
WORKING WITH YARN

To help you select colors for your projects, we have included numbers for Needloft® Plastic Canvas Yarn in our color keys. The headings in the color key are for Needloft® Yarn (**NL**) and the descriptive color name (**COLOR**). Needloft® Yarn is 100% nylon and is suitable only for 5 or 7 mesh plastic canvas.

Worsted weight yarn is used for most of the projects in this leaflet. Worsted weight yarn has four plies which are twisted together to form one strand. When the instructions indicate 2-ply yarn, separate the strand of yarn and stitch using only two of the four plies.

Needloft® Yarn will not easily separate. When the instructions call for 2-ply yarn, we recommend that you substitute with six strands of embroidery floss.

WORKING WITH PLASTIC CANVAS

Throughout this leaflet, the lines of the canvas will be referred to as threads. However, they are not actually "threads" since the canvas is nonwoven. To cut plastic canvas pieces accurately, count **threads** (not **holes**) as shown in **Fig. 1**.

Fig. 1

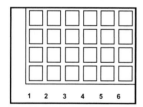

GENERAL INFORMATION

1. **Fig. 1** shows how to count threads accurately. Follow charts to cut out plastic canvas pieces.
2. Backstitches used for detail **(Fig. 5)**, French Knots **(Fig. 16, page 93)**, and Lazy Daisy Stitches **(Fig 19, page 93)** are worked over completed stitches.
3. Unless otherwise indicated, Overcast Stitches **(Fig. 21, page 94)** are used to cover edges of pieces and to join pieces.

STITCH DIAGRAMS

> **Unless otherwise indicated, bring threaded needle up at 1 and all odd numbers and down at 2 and all even numbers.**

ALICIA LACE STITCH

This series of stitches is worked in diagonal rows and forms a lacy pattern. Follow **Fig. 2** and work in one direction to cover every other diagonal row of intersections. Then work in the other direction **(Fig. 3)** to cover the remaining intersections.

Fig. 2

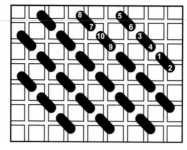

Fig. 3

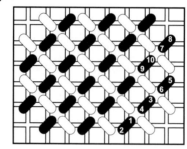

ALTERNATING MOSAIC STITCH

This three-stitch pattern forms small alternating squares as shown in **Fig. 4**.

Fig. 4

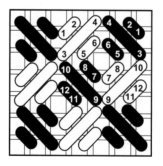

BACKSTITCH

This stitch is worked over completed stitches to outline or define **(Fig. 5)**. It is sometimes worked over more than one thread. Backstitch may also be used to cover canvas as shown in **Fig. 6**.

Fig. 5

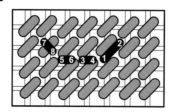

Fig. 6

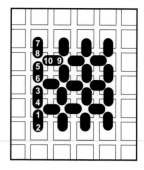

BRAIDED CROSS STITCH VARIATION

This stitch is used to cover the edge of the canvas. Begin by working stitches 1 through 3 as shown in **Fig. 7**. Starting with 4, proceed as shown in **Figs. 8** and **9**, working forward over three threads and back over two threads. It may be necessary to make extra stitches at the corners for better coverage.

Fig. 7

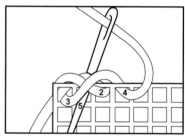

Fig. 8

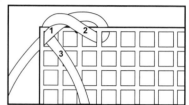

Fig. 9

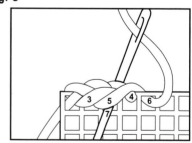

BULLION KNOT

Come up at 1; go down at 2, leaving a loop of yarn on top of the canvas. The distance between 1 and 2 is the length of the knot. Come up at 1 (**Fig. 10**). Wrap the loop around the needle as shown until the coil equals the distance between 1 and 2. Hold the coil in position while pulling the thread through (**Fig. 11**). As the thread is pulled taut, the coil will fold back over and lie on the canvas between 1 and 2. Secure knot by going down at 2 (**Fig. 12**).

Fig. 10

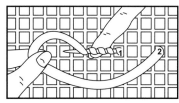

Fig. 11

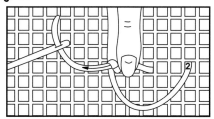

Fig. 12

CASHMERE STITCH

This rectangular stitch is formed by working four diagonal stitches as shown in **Fig. 13**.

Fig. 13

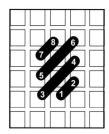

CROSS STITCH

This stitch is composed of two stitches (**Fig. 14**). The top stitch of each cross must always be made in the same direction. The number of intersections may vary according to the chart.

Fig. 14

FERN STITCH

Worked in horizontal rows, the Fern Stitch resembles a braid. Work stitches 1-4 as shown. Always working from left to right, continue as shown in **Fig. 15**. Length of first and last stitches of each row will vary according to chart.

Fig. 15

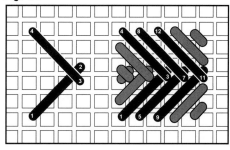

FRENCH KNOT

Bring needle up through hole. Wrap yarn once around needle and insert needle in same hole or adjacent hole, holding end of yarn with non-stitching fingers (**Fig. 16**). Tighten knot; then pull needle through canvas, holding yarn until it must be released.

Fig. 16

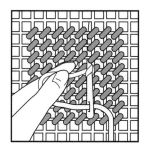

FRINGE

Fold a 12" length of yarn in half. Thread needle with loose ends of yarn. Take needle down at 1, leaving a 1" loop on top of the canvas. Come up at 2, bring needle through loop, and pull tightly (**Fig. 17**).

Fig. 17

GOBELIN STITCH

This basic straight stitch is worked over two or more threads or intersections. The number of threads or intersections may vary according to the chart (**Fig. 18**).

Fig. 18

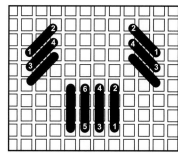

LAZY DAISY STITCH

Bring needle up at 1, make a loop and go down at 1 again (**Fig. 19**). Come up at 2, keeping yarn below needle's point. Pull needle through and secure loop by bringing yarn over loop and going down at 2.

Fig. 19

MOSAIC STITCH

This three-stitch pattern forms small squares (**Fig. 20**).

Fig. 20

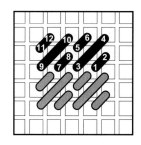

OVERCAST STITCH

This stitch covers the edge of the canvas and joins pieces of canvas (Fig. 21). It may be necessary to go through the same hole more than once to get an even coverage on the edge, especially at the corners.

Fig. 21

ROSE STITCH

To make a Rose, use a 48" length of yarn. Follow Fig. 22 to form a five spoke foundation. Bring needle up at 11 and weave yarn over and under spokes as shown in Fig. 23, keeping yarn tension loose. When spokes are covered, pull yarn slightly to puff Rose. With point of needle, pull up petals. Continue weaving until spokes are fully covered. Anchor yarn end on wrong side.

Fig. 22

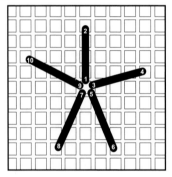

Fig. 23

SCOTCH STITCH

This stitch forms a square. It may be worked over three or more horizontal threads by three or more vertical threads. Fig. 24 shows it worked over three threads.

Fig. 24

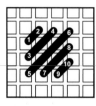

SEASHELL STITCH

This decorative stitch is composed of 15 stitches. Start at base of seashell and follow Fig. 25 to work stitches 1-10. Then follow Fig. 26 to work stitches 11-15.

Fig. 25

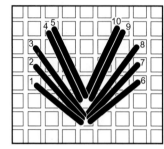

Fig. 26

SIX-TRIP HERRINGBONE STITCH

Six-Trip Herringbone Stitch is a woven stitch worked from left to right over four threads. Make first trip following Fig. 27. Using same color for second trip, work in adjacent spaces (Fig. 28). Work remaining four trips in same manner. Length of first and last stitch of each row will vary according to chart.

Fig. 27

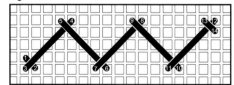

Fig. 28

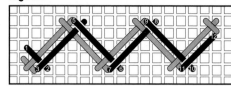

SMYRNA CROSS STITCH

This stitch is worked over two threads as a decorative stitch. Each stitch is worked completely before going on to the next (Fig. 29).

Fig. 29

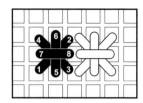

TENT STITCH

This stitch is worked in vertical or horizontal rows over one intersection as shown in Fig. 30.

Fig. 30

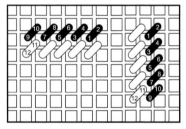

TURKEY LOOP STITCH

This stitch is composed of locked loops. Bring needle up through hole and back down through same hole, forming a loop on top of the canvas. A locking stitch is then made across the thread directly below or to either side of loop as shown in Fig. 31.

Fig. 31

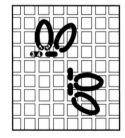

Instructions tested and photography items made by Janet Akins, Kandi Ashford, Kathleen Boyd, Virginia Cates, Carrie Clifford, Sharla Dunigan, JoAnn Forrest, Janice Gordon, Wanda Hopkins, Sadie Wilson, and Janie Wright.

INDEX

INDEX (Continued)